BITE SIZE PIECES

101 Thoughtful Nuggets
For a Happier,
More Successful
Life

Sam Spencer

Copyright 2011

ISBN 13: 978-1-938091-05-6

www.samspencer.us
bitesizepieces@samspencer.us

#1	LEARN TO LISTEN
#2	BE ON TIME
#3	WORK ON WHAT IS IMPORTANT
#4	GIVE FIVE MINUTES MORE
#5	DON'T PROCEED TO THE NEXT STEP BEFORE COMPLETING THE STEP YOU ARE ON
#6	SMILE AT OTHERS
#7	SING IN THE SHOWER
#8	HUG SOMEONE EACH DAY
#9	ELIMINATE INTEREST CHARGES
#10	EXERCISE REGULARLY
#11	EAT A GOOD DIET
#12	ELIMINATE JEALOUSY
#13	GIVE AN HONEST EFFORT
#14	BE PATIENT AND UNDERSTANDING
#15	APPRECIATE EVEN SMALL GROWTH
#16	DON'T BE AFRAID TO CHANGE LANES

#17	MAKE EACH DAY A GOOD DAY
#18	REMEMBER YOUR FAULTS BEFORE YOU BECOME ANGRY WITH OTHERS
#19	TREAT PEOPLE THE WAY THAT THEY WANT TO BE TREATED
#20	LET GO OF GUILT · QUIT FEELING GUILTY
#21	CONFER WITH OTHERS
#22	HAVE A QUIET PLACE
#23	FORGET THE PAST AND LOOK TOWARD THE FUTURE
#24	CARRY A SPARE TIRE
#25	THINK OF YOUR TANK AS HALF FULL
#26	WATCH YOURSELF PERFORM YOUR TASK
#27	LISTEN TO YOURSELF SPEAK TO OTHERS
#28	KNOW WHEN TO BACK UP
#29	CONTROL YOUR ENVIRONMENT
#30	SHAKE HANDS FIRMLY · LOOK THE OTHER PERSON IN THE EYE

#31	ONLY JUDGE YOURSELF AGAINST YOURSELF
#32	ADVERSITY IS THE BEST WAY TO GROW
#33	HAVE A MENTOR - IDOL - SOMEONE YOU CAN LEARN FROM
#34	KEEP YOUR LIFE SIMPLE
#35	CREATE GOOD HABITS TO REPLACE BAD HABITS
#36	ANALYZE THE NEXT STEP
#37	STOP SAYING "I CAN'T" AND START SAYING "HOW CAN I?"
#38	THINK YOUR PROJECT THROUGH AND ACT IT OUT
#39	ACT, DON'T RE-ACT
#40	ALWAYS BE WILLING TO LEARN
#41	REALIZE THAT OTHERS DON'T HAVE THE SAME PERSPECTIVE YOU DO
#42	PLAN AND PRACTICE YOUR RESPONSE AND SKILLS
#43	LEARN TO GOVERN YOURSELF

#44	IF YOU CANNOT DEPEND UPON YOURSELF, CAN OTHERS?
#45	ALL CHANGE COMES FROM WITHIN
#46	REALIZE YOU ARE THE MASTER OF YOUR DESTINY
#47	STAND AND FACE YOUR PROBLEMS
#48	TAKE THE INITIATIVE · JUST DO IT!
#49	LOOK FOR NEW IDEAS AND NEW OPPORTUNITIES
#50	GAIN AND CREATE WORTHWHILE EXPERIENCES
#51	LOOK FOR THE LESSON IN YOUR LIFE'S EXPERIENCE
#52	HELP OTHERS OBTAIN THEIR GOALS
#53	ASK A LOT OF QUESTIONS
#54	GAIN BALANCE IN YOUR LIFE
#55	NEVER QUIT · REALIGN · CHANGE FOCUS · CHANGE DEADLINES
#56	LEARN TO ACCEPT ALL PEOPLE
#57	LOOK FOR SOMETHING GOOD IN EVERYONE

#58	SAY SOMETHING GOOD ABOUT OTHERS
#59	DON'T PRE-JUDGE
#60	FORMULATE AN HONORABLE REASON WHY THEY ACTED AS THEY DID
#61	SAY "HELLO" TO STRANGERS
#62	BE COURTEOUS TO OTHERS
#63	REWARD YOURSELF
#64	TAKE TIME FOR YOURSELF
#65	RECOGNIZE THAT PROBLEMS ARE A PART OF LIFE - USE THEM TO GROW
#66	SLEEP ON IT AND LET THE SUBCONSCIOUS CREATE
#67	RECOGNIZE THE CONTRIBUTIONS OF OTHERS IN YOUR LIFE
#68	TAKE TIME TO SMELL THE ROSES
#69	TRY TO HAVE FUN
#70	ASK YOURSELF, "WHAT AM I SUPPOSE TO BE DOING HERE AND NOW?"

#	
#71	ACCENTUATE THE POSITIVE - LEARN FROM THE NEGATIVE
#72	ACT AND DRESS AS THE SITUATION REQUIRES
#73	DON'T SPEND IT UNTIL YOU HAVE EARNED IT
#74	PREPARE AND PLAN FOR PITFALLS
#75	TAKE A FEW MINUTES TO ASK "WHAT HAVE I LEARNED FROM THIS SITUATION?"
#76	SING AND LISTEN TO "FEEL GOOD" SONGS
#77	DON'T QUARREL WITH OTHERS
#78	HAVE A PLAN FOR EACH DAY, WEEK, MONTH, YEAR
#79	DO HARD THINGS FIRST
#80	GIVE FIVE MINUTES MORE
#81	LEARN TO SAY GOOD-BYE
#82	INVOLVE OTHERS TO REACH YOUR GOALS
#83	GIVE DAILY AFFIRMATIONS TO THOSE YOU LIVE WITH
#84	VISUALIZE SUCCESS
#85	LIVE WITH LESS THAN PERFECTION

#	
#86	RECOGNIZE YOU CAN'T SAVE THE WORLD
#87	STAY AWAY FROM NEGATIVE PEOPLE
#88	USE SELF TALK - GIVE YOURSELF DAILY AFFIRMATIONS
#89	HELP OTHERS SAVE FACE
#90	DON'T LOSE SIGHT OF YOUR OBJECTIVE
#91	LEARN SOMETHING NEW EACH DAY
#92	START EARLY IN THE MORNING
#93	LIVE YOUR DREAMS TODAY
#94	WORK HARDER AND SMARTER
#95	HELP MAKE OTHERS COMFORTABLE
#96	RECOGNIZE THAT THERE ARE SEVERAL WAYS TO ACHIEVE THE SAME RESULTS
#97	DON'T DWELL ON WHAT DIDN'T WORK
#98	LOOK IN THE MIRROR EACH DAY AND PRACTICE BEING NICE
#99	BE A PROBLEM SOLVER
#100	STOP SAYING "POOR ME" AND SAY "RICH ME"
#101	GIVE YOURSELF THE RESPECT YOU DESERVE

NOTE FROM THE AUTHOR

This book was designed with the person in mind who has a real desire to build a happier, more successful life. Who would like to reach new heights, wants to become his best, and who is interested in doing a little each day to become all he can be.

Take your time. After reading each page, stop to ponder what you have read. Visualize yourself exhibiting that particular characteristic in your daily affairs. As you do this, your creative abilities will provide ways that you personally can develop your own plan for success in whatever area you choose. This is your subconscious mind working to help you accomplish your desires. Give your subconscious a chance to help you. Since you become a product of your most dominating thoughts, keep the concepts you are working on foremost in your mind. That which is most easily visualized will be where you will have the most success. I suggest you start with those ideas first.

As you read this book you will find ideas that will stir you to immediate action. Others will not fit in your life today. Use the ideas presented here as building blocks in your life, building qualities, block by block, to make you the complete you. Work particularly with those concepts that will shape you into what you want to become.

Use this book as a reference for success, choosing the new, progressive habits you will introduce into your life. Work on those ideas that are relevant to your present needs and situation. When times change, you will too. Take time to refer to the titles again and again, choosing new areas that interest you and work the newly chosen behavior into your life.

Study each concept with an open and creative mind, always trying to think of ways you might incorporate it into your life. As you work on these goals, you will become a little happier and a little more successful each day, making you a whole lot happier and a whole lot more successful as time goes on. Keep moving forward! Never give up! Remember, even the slightest progress is worth celebrating!

Good luck!

Sam Spencer

INTRODUCTION

What a smorgasbord of opportunity life offers you, with so many avenues to choose from to direct your life. That's what makes life so exciting and fulfilling. You decide what you will do with your life. You decide how far you will go. You decide the characteristics, the traits, the things you will allow to influence your life to create your own unique individuality.

That is why I've written this book. I believe life is available to us in bite size pieces. You take the bite size pieces, develop them, and allow them to become a part of your life. You decide which pieces you will put on your own table, you even decide which bites you will take and which you will leave untouched. So piece by piece, step by step, you are literally becoming the product of all your every action.

How exciting! You and only you make the final choices. So many people allow others to make their choices, to rule their lives, to decide how they will feel, becoming intimidated to act in a certain way. Peer pressure becomes a factor in daily decisions: the clothes people wear, the places they go even the cars people drive. People worry what others think about them, "Am I good enough?" "Do I impress them favorably?"

Don't allow others to control your life. When you set a goal or make a choice, make certain that it is *your* choice, and that it is a *good* decision.

> You can become whatever you would like to be; if you have sufficient desire, acting on those things that will lead you to become that type of individual. Hence, life must be taken in "Bite Size Pieces." You have a lifetime to form this unique creation of self. Make it the best you can.

Create your own masterpiece.

THE MASTER SCULPTOR

I have a friend who is a sculptor. He demonstrated to me the way he created a bronze masterpiece. The first step was to envision what he was about to create. At times he would draw it on a piece of paper to preserve his idea, other times he would use a photo or postcard. Next he molded a piece of clay into the piece he wanted to create, carving and tooling with great detail. The clay model was then ready to have a mold made of it, soon to yield a bronze statue. The statue, however, was still rough with voids and imperfections.

After the bronze statue was pulled from the mold there was still an abundance of work left to be done to make it a great piece of art. The master then began to fill in the voids which the casting did not fill. Other areas had ridges from the mold which needed some fine grinding and delicate tooling. He sculpted until it was perfect. Every detail perfected, every flaw corrected and after many painstaking hours of dedicated and skillful effort the masterpiece was finished.

You are the master sculptor of your own life. You first decide what you will become. You may write this down on paper. You may leave the image of it in your own mind, but you decide what you will create. You begin to model and mold that which you envision, you may even try various avenues to see which fits you best. Choose and plan carefully. Remember, this is *you* that you are working on. Then, finally, after many years of dedication and hard work you have become a great masterpiece -- a legacy of your life.

Everyone learns and develops at different degrees. With this in mind, I have written this book so that each idea can be contemplated independently. You may link some together and work on several at one time. Also, to feel the joy of success, you don't have to do everything. You only have to succeed in one area to begin feeling better about yourself, and you will feel the joy of achieving something positive. Any real progress, no matter how small, should be celebrated; but don't stop there. Continue to press forward to even greater heights.

CONSIDER THIS AS ONE WAY TO USE THIS BOOK:

Read only the titles to familiarize yourself with the 101 ideas. Make a pencil mark by those that are especially interesting to you. Then read the information about those ideas. Pick only three to five ideas you prefer to work on. Remember that there is plenty of time to develop yourself. Also keep in mind that you may have a need to work on a particular idea but you are not ready. If you don't have sufficient desire you will only be wasting your time. Work on the desire, then on the idea. In the future as you read in this book, your attitudes may change. Ideas that did not appeal to you at one time may now be very important. That is what makes life so interesting. Life is always changing, giving you the opportunity to grow in new and exciting ways.

Once you have chosen the ideas that you will assimilate into your life, meditate on the information and visualize yourself achieving success in that area. As you do this, a plan of attack will begin to form in your mind. Write your plan down. Develop a way to implement the plan into your day, then work your plan.

PACE YOUR PROGRESS

Don't try to do everything all at once. Take little bits and pieces that you can incorporate into your life. These bits and pieces will enable you to have a happier, more abundant and successful life. People will enjoy being with you. You will enjoy being with others, and being a part of the world. You will learn to love life more, because you will make it fun as you incorporate these small success-focused ideas into your life.

Remember to run no faster than you are able, but KEEP RUNNING! These ideas are intended to help you keep on track, going in the right direction.

For the greatest success in personal development, become committed to the idea you have chosen to cultivate. Once you are happy with your progress in one area, move on to another. You may at one time have been very good at a particular skill, and, then as you glance at the book, you find that you have become rusty and need to brush up on it. Take time to do just that. Review the idea titles regularly. This will give you new feelings about ideas you brushed over in the past which, perhaps, are now more meaningful because of new experiences or changed circumstances.

101

THOUGHTFUL

NUGGETS

FOR A

HAPPIER,

MORE

SUCCESSFUL

LIFE

#1   LEARN TO LISTEN

Much can be learned from listening. Most people would rather talk than listen so it takes practice to learn to listen. Coach Lou Holtz said, "I never learned anything from talking, I only learn things from asking."

Let's rephrase that to say, "I never learned anything from talking, but I've learned many things by listening." By listening you gain the advantage of another's point of view. You can vicariously appreciate the various experiences of others. You may not have to experience the same lessons others learned from you listen well enough the first time. You will learn the motives of others, their problems, what stimulates them, and their opinions.

By listening intently you will learn what the real problems or objectives are of the other person. Failing to listen to the entire story will put you at a disadvantage. You may end up taking a wrong turn, promoting the wrong task or saying something you should not have said. This is a strenuous way to learn.

After making a conscientious effort to listen to my friends and family, I found that they began to talk to me more - especially my children. When you listen to others you develop a closer relationship, and a greater understanding of them. You will find that your problems and worries seem to diminish as you listen actively to others.

Set a goal today to sincerely listen more and speak less!

NUGGETS FOR THE MIND . . .

"The Art of conversation consists as much of listening politely as in talking agreeably."
 --George Atwell

"Most successful people I've known are the ones who do more listening than talking."
 --Bernard Baruch

"If you listen long enough you'll learn all you'll ever need to know!"
 --Sam Spencer

"The most important thing in communication is to hear what isn't being said."
 --Peter F. Drucker

"Nature has given us two eyes and two ears, and but one tongue, to the end that we should see and hear twice as much as we speak."
 --Socrates

"As I get older, I've learned to listen to people rather than accuse them of things."
 --Po Bronson

"If you only listen to what you want to hear, the rest will come back to haunt you."
 --Sam Spencer

#2   BE ON TIME

Some people are always late. If they realized that they are wasting someone else's time and stealing from their productivity -- maybe they would put forth a greater effort to be on time. You can't always be on time but you can usually be prompt. It has been said, "Punctuality is the politeness of kings." You must show others such politeness by being on time.

As you earn a reputation for being on time, people begin to count on you more and eventually trust takes over. Just this simple step to be on time can generate profound respect for you by others.

Thomas Jefferson said, "I owe all my success in life to having been a quarter hour before time." You don't have to always be fifteen minutes early, but if you were always five minutes early everywhere, even to work, what a great investment in yourself - and only for five minutes a day. Highly successful people will arrive early with collected thoughts and are ready to be productive.

On one occasion I had closed a sale after a lengthy interview. I hurried to my next appointment arriving almost 30 minutes late. At the door I introduced myself and apologized for being late. The woman reproved me and said she would not do business with someone who could not be counted on! My competitor got the sale which I could have had.

When you cause others to wait for you, it can be like stealing, stealing the time they may have reserved for their families or perhaps something else. BE ON TIME!

NUGGETS FOR THE MIND . . .

"Unfaithfulness in the keeping of an appointment is an act of clear dishonesty. You may as well borrow a person's money as his time."
 --Horace Mann

"Punctuality is one of the cardinal business virtues: always insist on it in your subordinates."
 --Don Marquis

"Success waits for no man."
 --Author Unknown

"I could never think well of a man's intellectual or moral character, if he was habitually unfaithful to his appointments."
 --Nathaniel Emmons

"Lost yesterday, somewhere between sunrise and sunset, two golden hours, each set with sixty diamond minutes. No reward is offered for they are gone forever."
 --Horace Mann

"Opportunities are like sunrises. If you wait too long, you miss them."
 -- William Arthur Ward

"Success will always arrive at it's own appointed time, make sure *you* are there to greet it!"
 --Sam Spencer

#3   WORK ON WHAT IS IMPORTANT

Everyday you have choices of what to work on. To a great extent you determine how you will spend much of your time. It's very easy to decide to work on what you like to do first. Sometimes this might be okay. To achieve greater success, however, often the best approach is to decide to work on what is most important first. Sooner or later you will have to do what is important. If you make it a point to do the important things first they will always be done in time.

You will have to decide what is important. Practice and daily appraisal of what you have to do is the first step. Simply make a list of your tasks, number them from the most important to the least important, then do the most important first. If you don't get everything done, for whatever reason, you will at least have the most important things already completed.

I make three lists. One, the things I must do right away. Two, the things that would be good to get done shortly. And three, the things that can be done anytime. I then work each list into my schedule starting with the "must do" items first.

Make a goal to work on what is important. You will find yourself having less stress. You will not be worried about when you will get it done, it will already be in your plan.

NUGGETS FOR THE MIND . . .

"The "Extra Mile" will have no traffic jams.
--Author Unknown

> Look up and not down;
> Look forward and not back;
> Look out and not in;
> Lend a Hand.

--Edward Everett Hale, Lend a Hand Society.

"The demands on our time are either important or unimportant, urgent or not urgent. Important things serve your mission; unimportant things don't."
--Steven R. Covey

"When a person is down in the world, an ounce of help is better than a pound of preaching."
--Edward Bulwer-Lytton

"When a man forgets himself he usually does something everybody else remembers."
--James Eno

"Our rewards in life will always be in exact proportion to our service."
--Earl Nightingale

"If people concentrated on the really important things in life, there'd be a shortage of fishing poles."
--Doug Larson

#4   DO AWAY WITH FEAR

Fear can stop progress. Most of the time fear is induced because of a lack of knowledge, understanding or trust. One of the popular thrills of today is bungee jumping. When you understand that the cord is made up of many cords, that it is securely fastened to the tower on one end and to yourself on the other, and also become familiar with the safety measures taken, then your fear diminishes. The more knowledge, understanding and trust you have, the less fear you will have, and your progress will not be impeded.

A man who worked for me was afraid of heights. We were washing some tanker trucks, and it was necessary to get on top of the catwalk of the tanker to brush the sides.

All morning I had been the one working on the top. Not knowing his fear, I asked him to get on the catwalk and take a turn. He slowly climbed to the top and cautiously leaned over to brush the sides. He finished the work and quickly came down. Once his feet were on the ground, with beads of sweat covering his face, he expressed his fear. I really admired his courage and invited him to work on the ground. By his choice, he continued to do more work on top to help him deal with his fear. When he got on top and saw the safety rails, this knowledge relaxed his fear. Through practice it enabled him to go past his fear. Knowledge gives you power to overcome fear. My friend's progress was not stopped by the roadblock of fear, he just stepped to the side and went around it. You can do the same.

NUGGETS FOR THE MIND . . .

"Let me assert my firm belief that the only thing we have to fear is fear itself, nameless, unreasoning, unjustified terror which paralyzes needed efforts to convert retreat into advance."
  --Franklin D. Roosevelt

"Nothing is so much to be feared as fear."
  --Henry David Thoreau

"Fear always springs from ignorance."
  --Ralph Waldo Emerson

"Nothing is terrible but fear itself."
  --Francis Bacon

"The greatest mistake you can make in life is to be continually fearing that you will make one."
  --Author Unknown

"We must get rid of fear; we cannot act at all till then. A man's acts are slavish, not true but specious; his very thoughts are false, he thinks too as a slave and coward, till he has got fear under his feet."
  --Thomas Carlyle

"Fear is just excitement in need of an attitude adjustment."
  --Russ Quaglia

#5 DON'T PROCEED TO THE NEXT STEP BEFORE COMPLETING THE STEP YOU ARE ON

It is important to look forward to the next level; this is a healthy, progressive attitude that breeds success. However, you really cannot go to the next level of achievement until you have completed the one you are on. To prematurely advance to the next step will almost inevitably require that you go back and complete the level you were on.

Order is the key. Once you have established the steps necessary to get you where you're headed, follow your plan. Complete each task before you move on to the next task. You would not put the roof on a house until you have built the structure to support it. It is the same with your life. Complete the foundation to support your life, then the structure followed by the roof. Study your next step and know where you are going. This could be education, working on a specific idea, saving for a home, or even one of the ideas in this book. Once you have identified your next step, work on it until it is finished, then move on!

Thus you learn order, patience and self-discipline. All are virtues, that lead to a happier, more successful you.

NUGGETS FOR THE MIND . . .

"If we cross the bridge before we finish building it, we will soon find ourselves in the river below."
--Sam Spencer

"Our patience will achieve more than our force."
--Edmund Burke

"No thing great is created suddenly, anymore than a bunch of grapes or a fig. If you tell me that you desire a fig, I answer you that there must be time. Let it first blossom, then bear fruit, then ripen." --Epictetus

"Patience is waiting. Not passively waiting. That is laziness. But to keep going when the going is hard and slow -- that is patience."
--Author Unknown

"You don't just luck into things as much as you'd like to think you do. You build step by step, whether it's friendships or opportunities."
--Barbara Bush

"And step by step, since time began, I see the steady gain of man.
--John Greenleaf Whittier

#6 SMILE AT OTHERS

There is no richer way to make others feel better or happier about themselves than to smile at them. A smile is so powerful. It not only effects the person you are smiling at, but it lifts your spirit as well.

On a recent trip out of town I decided to make it a point to smile at everyone with whom I made eye contact. What an incredible experience I had. My day was progressively more electrifying. In fact just smiling started some conversations that became genuinely rewarding. When you smile at others they will smile back.

You may never know, you could be the only person who smiled at that person all day. Smiling is contagious, you brighten the day of others when you smile at them, you become happier and more fulfilled. They now smile at some one else, soon one smile will have made many people happy. Just think, this all started with you!

Mark Twain said, "The best way to cheer yourself up is to cheer somebody else up." How true! When you smile at another person, two hearts are filled. Try it!

CHANGE
If a simple smile you add,
To ev'n a small exchange,
Cheer you'll give unto the sad,
And always, leave with change.
---- Sam Spencer

NUGGETS FOR THE MIND . . .

"Nothing on earth can smile but man. Gems may flash reflected light; but what is a diamond flash compared with an eye flash? Flowers cannot smile; this is a charm that even they cannot claim. It is the prerogative of man; it is the color which love wears; and cheerfulness and joy -- these three."
 --Henry Ward Beecher

"The men whom I have seen succeed best in life always have been cheerful and hopeful men; who went about their business with a smile on their faces; and took the changes and chances of this mortal life like men; facing rough and smooth alike as it came."
 --Charles Kingsley

"A Smile is the second best thing to do with your lips."
 --Anita Hallman

"You're never fully dressed until you put a smile on."
 --Author Unknown

"I love the man who can smile in trouble, and who can gather strength from distress, and grow brave by reflection."
 --Thomas Paine

"There are hundreds of languages in the world but a smile speaks them all."
 --Author Unknown

#7   SING IN THE SHOWER

This may seem silly, but it really works to brighten and energize your day. I am not a great singer, nor am I even an average singer. But when I sing my spirit is lifted. I feel as though I want to succeed, I want to go places and do things. I have more enthusiasm for life. It may very well be that 30 minutes after you get out of the shower something negative happens. When you get into this habit, your spurts of happiness and enjoyment will last a little longer. The negative will become short lived. You will become a happier and more positive person, not to ignore the fact that you started your day out in a cheerful way.

One morning I had awakened much earlier than usual. Frustrated by not being able to fall back asleep, I finally jumped into a nice warm shower and really soaked it up. While soaking I began to sing one of my favorite songs that usually inspires me. I got out of the shower with great enthusiasm, dressed and went into the garage looking for something fun to do until my family got up. Soon I found myself involved in a task that I had put off for several months. Quickly I was sailing through this otherwise distasteful task, still singing my song. After an hour and a half I finished the job and went back into the house. As I sat eating breakfast, I began to laugh because I realized that I had motivated myself to action, doing the very things I had often preached to others.

To me it was funny to have unknowingly motivated myself into doing a task that I had put off for a very long time and I truthfully enjoyed the entire job. And to think, it all started with singing in the shower!

NUGGETS FOR THE MIND . . .

"Cheerfulness is an excellent wearing quality. It has been called the bright weather of the heart. It gives harmony of soul and is a perpetual song without words. It is tantamount to repose. It enables nature to recruit its strength."
  -- Samuel Smiles

"Cheerfulness in most people, is the rich and satisfying results of strenuous discipline."
  --Edwin Percy Whipple

"A cheerful man is one who can present a smiling face to every turn of fortune; not one whose radiance is skin-deep and disappears when shares are down or dinner is a trifle late."
  --Leigh Smith

"Wondrous is the strength of cheerfulness, and its power of endurance -- the cheerful man will do more in the same time, will do it better, will preserve it longer, than the sad or sullen."
  --Thomas Carlyle

#8   HUG SOMEONE EACH DAY

This is a tough one, especially for most men. Men generally find it difficult to hug special people, let alone just good friends. Have you ever had someone put their arm around you and ask you how you were doing? How did you feel? I'll tell you how you most likely felt. You felt accepted. You felt a part of someone's life. You felt important. You felt like someone truly cared. Now you should try it. You will make a difference in someone's life, especially those whom you see have had a tough day or someone who has done a good job. This hug doesn't have to be a big embrace. It can be as simple as an arm around the shoulder, with a few sincere words, or like two old pals walking off the playing field, arm on shoulder. Most of us did this when we were young and it made us happier and closer. Why not do it now? It will have the same effect on you today!

Often we instinctively put up a barrier which says, "I don't know if I can trust you." Somehow this sincere touching breaks down barriers. People typically respond favorably. They will lower their barricades of resistance. You will find they will be more prone to share with you and you could even gain a trusted and valued friend.

When we treat others with this type of genuine concern, we make them feel a little better. It rubs off on us and we, also, feel better and more fulfilled. Such a simple way to have a happier life. Try it at home! Try it at work! Try it with your friends!

NUGGETS FOR THE MIND . . .

"The best thing to give to your enemy is forgiveness; to an opponent, tolerance; to a friend, your heart; to your child, a good example; to a father, deference; to your mother, conduct that will make her proud of you; to yourself, respect; to all men, charity."
 --Mrs. Balfour

"A good deed is never lost. He who sows courtesy, reaps friendship; he who plants kindness, gathers love; pleasure bestowed upon a grateful mind was never sterile, but generally gratitude begets reward."
 --Basil

"The only way to have a friend is to be one."
 --Ralph Waldo Emerson

"When good friends walk beside us
On the trails that we must keep,
Our burdens seem less heavy
And the hills are not so steep.
The weary miles pass swiftly
Taken in a joyous stride,
And all the world seems brighter
When friends walk by our side."
 --Author Unknown

#9   ELIMINATE INTEREST CHARGES

This is an economic idea to help you become more successful. There are so many wonderful items available to us in the world today. Nice cars, beautiful homes, entertainment, etc. Total the interest you pay each year. Look at each source carefully. Eliminate the absolute necessities, then review the balance. What difference would this extra money make in your life? Wouldn't you rather invest it in yourself than invest it in your banker?

Give yourself a raise! Eliminating unnecessary interest in your life. I devised a plan to eliminate all the interest from my life over a four year period. After faithfully implementing the plan - success! What a difference it made for me. I now need thousands less each year to live on and have more cash for myself.

When you owe anyone, you are in a type of bondage, servitude to that person, even if they might be family or a really good friend. You will never experience true freedom until you eliminate from your life, the interest you pay to others.

Self discipline, and the ability to live beneath your means, is the only way you can truly accumulate wealth. We must do with less today if we are to have more for tomorrow. Take a lesson from the ant who is always working today to prepare and save for tomorrow.

NUGGETS FOR THE MIND . . .

"As an individual who undertakes to live by borrowing, soon finds his original means devoured by interest, and next no one left to borrow from -- so must it be with a government."
 --Abraham Lincoln

"Usury is the certainest means of gain, though one of the worst; as that whereby a man doth eat his bread with sweat of another's face, and besides, doth plough upon Sundays."
 --Francis Bacon

"Happy the man who far from schemes of business, like the early generations of mankind, works his ancestral acres with oxen of his own breeding, from all usury free."
 --Horace [Quintas Horatius Flaccus]

"A principal rule of life is to eliminate interest"
 --Sam Spencer

"Money talks, -- But credit has an echo."
 --Author Unknown

"Too many people spend money they haven't earned, to buy things they don't want, to impress people they don't like."
 --Will Rogers

"If you have an education about how money works, you gain power over it and can begin building wealth."
 --Robert T. Kiyosaki

#10 EXERCISE REGULARLY

You own a very powerful piece of equipment, this human body of yours. Great power physically. Great power mentally. Great power emotionally, and great power spiritually. You can do countless great things when you put your mind to it.

Exercising regularly helps you to be sharp on your feet. Keeping the heart in good shape, and your muscles toned will keep you ready to go the extra mile when necessary. Nobody will need to carry you. You will be able to carry your own weight.

One thing you can do is take the stairway rather than the elevator. You've heard this before, but now do it! Walk, if it is close enough. When you travel, get a room above the 10th floor and then walk up the stairs. Do this and you will have more energy and stamina. When shopping park far enough away to get in a little walk.

You have heard all of this before, but it's time to get serious. Think of ways you can walk more, and do it briskly. Be creative! Jump rope in the garage. Get on the trampoline with your children. Ride a bike. Walk around the block. Take a day hike. There are many ways to get exercise, but know that you need some good exercise to have a happier more successful life!

NUGGETS FOR THE MIND...

"Every man is the builder of a temple, called his body."
--Henry David Thoreau

"Conquer thyself. Till thou hast done that; thou art a slave; for it is almost as well to be in subjection to another's appetite as thine own."
--Burton

"How shall I be able to rule over others, that have not full power and command of myself?"
--Francois Rabelais

"A journey of a thousand miles must begin with a single step."
--Chinese Proverb

"Those who think they have not time for bodily exercise will sooner or later have to find time for illness."
--Edward Stanley

"A man too busy to take care of his health is like a mechanic too busy to take care of his tools."
--Spanish Proverb

#11   EAT A GOOD DIET

How would it be if the government regulated your body as they do motor vehicles? Each year on your birthday you would have to report to a government license station. There you would have a safety inspection to see if you had performed all the necessary maintenance your body required in the past year. They would require that you get everything in order and tuned-up before you got a license to operate yourself for the next year. Since they don't, you must do this yourselves!

Do you allow the most valuable piece of equipment you own to be fed garbage? Do you allow it to sit and deteriorate?

What would happen if:
...you treated your tools at work the same way you treat your body?
...you left your computer terminal out in the rain?
...you left your saw sitting in the mud waiting to be used again?
...your sewing machine was left exposed to dust?

When you consider that your body has the capacity to produce immeasurable income and has unlimited potential for performing good works, it seems absurd to administer anything but the best care, in every way, to your irreplaceable body. Realize the importance of eating right to stay well and be productive. Make a commitment to both exercise regularly and eat wisely.

Dump the garbage habit if you are its victim!

NUGGETS FOR THE MIND . . .

"A sense of purpose and the opportunity to contribute to others -- these are as vital to total health as are adequate nutrition and rest."
 --H. A. Holle, M. D.

"For the sake of health, medicines are taken by weight and measure; so ought food to be, or by some similar rule"
 --Skelton

"Animals feed; man eats. Only the man of intellect and judgment knows how to eat."
 --Savarin

"The only way to keep your health is to eat what you don't want, drink what you don't like, and do what you'd rather not."
 --Mark Twain

"There's a lot of people in this world who spend so much time watching their health that they haven't the time to enjoy it."
 --Josh Billings

#12 ELIMINATE JEALOUSY

Jealousy is one of those negative traits that makes someone unpleasant to be around. Jealous people are always wanting more than they have, wanting what other people have. To eliminate jealousy, you must accept yourself as you are. Be honest with your abilities, talents and needs. You need to learn to be happy with what you have. Change the way you look at others, by not looking at them as having more, but only as having other things.

When you spend your time worrying about what others have, you are burning vital energy that could motivate you and propel you to greater success. Here are five ideas to help you eliminate jealousy:

...Learn to say "I am glad they have what they have."
...Look at others as having different abilities, possessions, and talents than you.
...Learn to be happy with what you are and what you have.
...Always do your best and know that you are doing your best.
...Learn to love unconditionally.

Jealousy can be like a cancer, not only does it have the potential destroy relationships, but it can ultimately destroy you.

Set some definite goals to help on this one!

NUGGETS FOR THE MIND . . .

"Jealousy, the jaundice of the soul."
--John Dryden

"Envy always implies conscious inferiority wherever it resides."
--Plutarch

"Envy shoots at others, and wounds herself."
--Swedish Proverb

"Jealousy is all the fun you think they had."
--Erica Jong

"Lots of people know a good thing the minute the other fellow sees it first."
--Job E. Hodges

"Jealousy is ... a tiger that tears not only its prey but also its own raging heart."
--Michael Beer

"The truest mark of being born with great qualities, is being born without envy. "
--François, Duc de La Rochefoucauld

#13   GIVE AN HONEST EFFORT

What is an honest effort? You will have to answer this one yourself, but I will give you some guidelines to consider:

> ...Are you putting your best foot forward in everything you do?
> ...At work are you using all the skills you have?
> ...In your dealings with others are you genuine?
> ...At the end of each task, each day, ask yourself;
>   "Have I given my best to this task?"

Honesty builds character! The above qualities identify you as a person to be relied upon. As people establish trust in you, you will feel a greater degree of self-worth, leading to a happier life.

I believe you cannot be truly happy unless you feel that you have given your best. You never have to hang your head low if you gave your very best even though you still come short of the mark. To have given your very best and failed displays more integrity than giving a partial effort and coming in first.

You will always know if you are giving an honest effort. When I give an honest effort I feel fulfilled. You, too, will experience the same feelings by knowing you have given your best.

NUGGETS FOR THE MIND...

"Being entirely honest with oneself is a good exercise."
--Sigmund Freud

"Thank God every morning when you get up that you have something to do that day which must be done; whether you like it or not. Being forced to work and forced to do your best will breed in you temperance and self control; diligence and strength of will; cheerfulness and content; and a hundred virtues which the idle never know."
--Charles Kingsley

"My father believed that there was no point in worrying about whether you succeeded or failed at a job, as long as you were sure that you had done your best."
--Margaret Truman

"Do your best every minute -- you never know when someone is taking your measure for a better position."
--Author Unknown

"I have nothing to offer but blood, toil and sweat."
--Winston Churchill

"If a job is worth doing at all, it's worth doing well."
--My Mother and Your Mother

#14 BE PATIENT AND UNDERSTANDING

Patience takes a constant effort. Many times you need to bite your tongue, hold yourself back and begin to count. You must realize that patience comes through understanding. When you work on patience, you must also work on understanding because they go hand in hand.

To help develop patience and understanding, here are some questions to ask yourself:

...Why did they do that?
...Did I give them enough time to perform the task?
...Did they understand the instructions they received?
...What is the basic knowledge level required?
...How did my peers and I perform in the same situation?

As you take time to consider these questions, patience and understanding will surely increase.

If you truly want to learn patience, I suggest you work with teenagers as they feel their way through life, remembering your struggles on the way!

Look back in your life experiences and see from whence you came and then look at where you are now. Look at others and see what they have accomplished. You will then appreciate how important patience and understanding are.

NUGGETS FOR THE MIND...

"I hear and I forget. I see and I remember. I do and I understand."
--Chinese Philosophy

"Do not laugh, do not weep, try to understand."
--Benedict Spinoza

"Everything comes to him who hustles while he waits."
--Thomas A. Edison

"Patience is a minor form of despair, disguised as a virtue"
--Ambrose Bierce

"Patience is power; with time and patience the mulberry leaf becomes silk."
--Chinese Proverb

"A Recipe to recover lost patience:
When you have lost your patience count to 100. If you haven't found your patience by the time you reach 100... Repeat the above step until you find it."
--Sam Spencer

#15 APPRECIATE EVEN SMALL GROWTH

Growth is very important, but equally important is the ability to recognize growth! If you are not growing, you are going in reverse.

Abraham Lincoln said, "I walk slowly, but I never go backwards." A river may slowly make its way to the ocean, or it may make its way in a torrent; nevertheless, both will get to the ocean. If you are on a diet and lose only one pound this week, celebrate! You're going in the right direction! Your goal may have been five pounds. But if you miss your goal, even though you did your best, do you quit because you came short? Do you stop everything? Do you throw away your effort? No! You celebrate what you have accomplished and you continue to go forward!

Maybe your goal was too challenging to start with and now you have a more realistic vision. Change the time frame to achieve, but don't change the goal. Once again, appreciate even small growth and go onward.

Remember that a beautiful brick home is built one brick at a time. Recognize the progress as you lay each brick in your life. (NOTE: Allow others this same benefit too.)

Here is a stimulating activity. Climb a flight of stairs. Start one step at a time and with each step praise yourself saying; "Great work! Good job! Fantastic!" Soon you will be taking the steps briskly and even two at a time. Experience the joy of accomplishment, one step at a time.

NUGGETS FOR THE MIND...

"No act of kindness, no matter how small, is ever wasted."
--Aesop

"In all the affairs of life; social as well as political; courtesies of a small and trivial character are the ones which strike deepest to the grateful and appreciating heart."
--Henry Clay

"Nothing is particularly hard if you divide it into small jobs."
--Henry Ford

"Has not God borne with you these many years? Be ye tolerant of others."
--Hosea Ballou

"I was taught that the way of progress is neither swift nor easy. "
--Madame Marie Curie

"Never discourage anyone who continually makes progress, no matter how slow."
--Plato

#16 DON'T BE AFRAID TO CHANGE LANES

It has been said, "Perfection is immutable, but for things imperfect, to change is the way to perfect them." Change takes you to new worlds. Look forward to change. All around you every day things are in a constant mode of change. Each day you wait anxiously to see the new flowers. Has it rained? Did it snow? Is the wind blowing? Sir Edmund Burke said, "You must all obey the great law of change. It is the most powerful law of nature." As you resist change the world passes you by, you miss exciting new challenges and opportunities for success and growth.

Just as you think you are on top of things, life offers you little detours. Don't be afraid of the detours. Others have taken these same roads; you can learn from them. Few are lost by the wayside unless of course, they give up. Some journeys will take more time than others, some may have greater challenges, but have the courage to continue to the end. That is where you will find the reward.

To have a happier life you need to realize and accept that change, setbacks and detours are inevitable. On the way to a most important job interview you have car trouble and are delayed. You are running late and the elderly gentleman in front of you is especially slow. This can certainly spoil your day unless you comprehend that the unexpected is typically normal.

So go ahead and change lanes...you may find the going smoother.

NUGGETS FOR THE MIND . . .

"Any man who is unable to change his method and adapt himself to change of conditions, because of closed-mindedness toward progressive improvement and development, lacks ambition. He is dead mentally because his mind is locked or tightly closed against doing anything different. The things we close minds against today may be taken for granted tomorrow."   --Walter Dill Scott

"The pessimist complains about the wind; the optimist expects it to change; the realist adjusts the sail."   --William Arthur Ward

"He who rejects change is the architect of decay. The only human institution which rejects progress is the cemetery."
 --Prime Minister Harold Wilson

"Everything is in a state of change. Thou, thyself art in everlasting change and in corruption to correspond, so is the whole universe."
--Marcus Aurelius

"Just remember that all this abnormality is only normal."
 --Sam Spencer

#17   MAKE EACH DAY A GOOD DAY

Someone once said, "Instead of 'have a good day' -- 'Make it a good day.'" You have the ability to decide what you are going to do with your day. Everyday there are events in your life that can turn your day positive or negative. It is how you handle these events that determine what kind of a day you will have.

Imagine you may have an experience such as running out of gas in your car. This could ruin your whole day, if you choose to let it. Say to yourself---"These things happen, I'll correct the problem and get on my way." It may not be fun at the time, but don't let it ruin your day. Look ahead to the rest of the day, forget the past. It is gone you cannot change the past. Cheerfully go forward looking toward the future. Do this and tomorrow your memories of the past will be enriched.

You make the choice to be happy or unhappy, you choose to be angry or not, you choose how you will let life's daily events affected you and to what extent. Begin each day with a conscious choice to make it a happier day and you will be developing a habit that will make each day much more pleasant and positive.

Here's a small piece of advice: Always have a few tasks that you can look forward to doing strategically placed throughout your day.

NUGGETS FOR THE MIND . . .

"Your outlook determines your future."
--Norman Vincent Peale

"If you keep saying things are going to be bad, you have a good chance to be a prophet."
--Isaac Bashevis Singer

"If you treat every situation as a life and death matter, you'll die a lot of times."
--Author Unknown

"They who know how to employ opportunities will often find that they can create them; and what we can achieve depends less on the amount of time we possess than on the use we make oftime."
--John Stuart Mill

"Nothing is so responsible for the good old days as a bad memory.
--Franklin Delano Roosevelt

"Everything can be taken from a man but one thing; the last of the human freedoms—to choose one's attitude in any given set of circumstances, to choose one's own way."
--Victor E. Frankl

#18 REMEMBER YOUR FAULTS BEFORE YOU BECOME ANGRY WITH OTHERS

One day while my wife was driving home, the car ran out of gas. As I drove home I noticed her car parked at the side of the road. My first thoughts were of the two occasions that day when I reminded her that the car needed gas. I began to mentally rehearse the words I might say to mock this unfortunate event. As I roll-played this mental dialogue I began to think how she might respond to the embarrassment and hurt feelings this would cause. Then I remembered that I too had performed this same absentminded stunt. I relived my own embarrassment at my oversights. Upon arriving at the house, I found the gas can and without a word retrieved her car. No words were needed, I had been there before. It was best to solve the problem without contempt.

Make this a habit by thinking to yourself, "What have I done that was similar to this?" "How did I feel?" Take time for some introspection and don't let your anger and emotion control your actions. Take time to think and feel as the other person might feel. Develop empathy

If you remember your own faults when you correct others, your correcting will be done more gently. Counseling will be done with kindness and that is always more effective.

NUGGETS FOR THE MIND...

"The real fault is to have faults and not try to amend them."
 --Confucius

"We spotlight the faults of others as they parade before us while we safeguard our own."
 --Sam Spencer

"He who has nothing but virtues is not much better than he who has nothing but faults."
 --Swedish Proverb

"A fault that humbles a man is of greater value than a virtue that puffs him up."
 --Author Unknown

"Quarrels would not last long if faults were only on one side."
 --Francois, Duc de la Rochefoucauld

"Admit errors; make apologies; clear up the brooding clouds at home and in the heart that keep us from enjoying life and loved ones, and from being at peace with ourselves inside."
 --Richard L. Evans

#19 TREAT PEOPLE THE WAY THEY WANT TO BE TREATED

I have heard of a platinum rule which says, "Do unto others as they would have you do unto them." Think about it -- if you want people to respond, then treat them with the respect they deserve, treat them with the kindness that they would like.

When I was 20 years old and living in Venezuela, each morning I would leave my apartment and walk to work across a certain bridge. On occasion I would meet someone who absolutely did not like Americans. This was one of those occasions. The man was a plumber. He walked the streets with a wooden box full of his plumbing tools offering his services calling; "Plomero, Plomero." One day as I crossed the bridge he began to chase me yelling "Yankee go home." I hustled to outrun him and especially the pipe wrench he was shaking. This continued for several days. Then I decided to try saying something nice to him. For the next several mornings as he went through his ritual, I wished him a nice day from the other side of the street as I hurried on. Progressively he became less rude as we passed. I continued to be polite and respectful, wishing him a nice day. In about a two week period the man completely changed. He no longer was rude. His hostility had disappeared. I believe that the change came about because he was treated with the respect that all people deserve.

To treat people the way they would like to be treated you will have to know something about their inner feelings, goals, needs and desires. You will need to have some genuine level of interest in them.

NUGGETS FOR THE MIND...

"I expect to pass through this world but once. Any good work, therefore, any kindness, or any service I can render to any soul of man or animal, let me do it now! Let me not neglect or defer it, for I shall not pass this way again."
  --Thomas Carlyle

"It is a good and safe rule to sojourn in every place as if you meant to spend your life there; never omitting an opportunity of doing a kindness; or speaking a true word; or making a friend."
  --John Ruskin

"Life is too short for words that hurt; For subtle thrusts and for phrases curt; For motives unkind and sharp retort -- For any of these -- life is too short."   --Lucile Veneklasen

"Trust men, and they will be true to you; treat them gently, and they will show themselves great."
  --Ralph Waldo Emerson

"Treat people as if they were what they ought to be and you help them to become what they are capable of being."
  --Goethe

#20   LET GO OF GUILT - QUIT FEELING GUILTY

You might ask, "Why do away with guilt?" Easy answer. Once you have learned from the problem and made the problem right, guilt only makes you miserable. Guilt is negative. It cannot build; it only tears down. It snowballs in your life by railing against you for not doing enough, not having enough time, not being as perfect as you think others want you to be or, even worse, not being able to be as perfect as you expect yourself to be.

It doesn't matter how perfectly the lady down the street keeps her house; you have no need to feel guilty that you cannot do the same. Is her house ever dirty? Probably! Even those who appear to always do the right thing, or are always in the right place at the right time also, on occasion, fall short. Cut yourself some slack. Here are some ideas to help break the guilt cycle.

...Forgive yourself and forgive others.
...Accept the facts, change what you can, accept the rest.
...Think about something positive, different and uplifting.
...Review your goals and self-expectation. They may be too lofty.
...Be honest about your abilities, yet be all you can be.

Take responsibility for your actions, but don't let guilt rule your life. LET IT GO!

NUGGETS FOR THE MIND . . .

"How blunt are all the arrows of adversity in comparison with those of guilt!"
 --Blair

"There is no witness so dreadful, no accuser so terrible as the conscience that dwells in the heart of every man." -- Polybius

Guilt: The gift that keeps on giving"
 --Erma Bombeck

"The devil seeketh that all men might be miserable like unto himself"
 -- Book Of Mormon

"There is no peace on earth today save the peace in the heart at home with God... No man can be at peace with his neighbor who is not at peace with himself."
 --Edna St. Vincent Millay

"There's no problem so awful that you can't add some guilt to it and make it even worse!"
 --Schulz

#21 CONFER WITH OTHERS

Nobody has all the answers. Lawyers think they do, politicians say they do, and salesman act like they do, but nobody has all the answers.

I am always seeking advice and solutions from others who have been successful and have more knowledge than I do. This has always been an important key to my personal success. Conferring with others not only helps me to analyze my next step, but helps me to predict the results. Another thing I do is to show others what I am doing and ask them how I might improve. These can be powerful and informative meetings. It is like having your own personal trainer.

When I built my own house, there were many aspects I was not at all acquainted with and others I had done only once. I did not have the knowledge to build a house without occasional direction and help from others. Every few days I would visit one of my friends who was a builder by profession. We would discuss where I was in the construction process and I would ask questions. My friend would then instruct me about the next step and tutor me on how to do it correctly. I would return and implement my new knowledge. If it were not for the help of others I never could have accomplished that monumental task.

When you are able to put your goals ahead of your pride you will accomplish considerably more and you will open the door to unlimited knowledge as you confer with others. Analyze the input, determine what will work for you, and then use it.

NUGGETS FOR THE MIND . . .

"Good counsels observed are chains of grace."
  --Fuller

"They that won't be counseled can't be helped."
  --Benjamin Franklin

"Works of the intellect are great only by comparison with each other."
  --Ralph Waldo Emerson

"Old people love to give good advice; it compensates them for their inability to set a bad example."
  --Duc de La Rochefoucauld

"The greatest trust between man and man is the trust of giving counsel."
  --Bacon

"He who calls in the aid of an equal understanding doubles his own; and he who profits by a superior understanding raises his powers to a level with the height of the superior understanding he unites with."
  --Burke

#22 HAVE A QUIET PLACE

A quiet place is a place where you can go, be away from the world, meditate, write, think, or just to be alone. This doesn't have to be some exotic or remote location. It just need only to be a place that is sacred especially to you, a place where you can go for a few minutes and gather your thoughts. The purpose of your quiet place, or places, is to allow you time to think unrestricted and uninterrupted by the distractions of the world and your environment. A place where you feel comfortable, relaxed and free.

I have a friend who takes his lunch break in his car away from the lunch room and others. He reads, reflects and has a quiet time for himself. His friends probably think he is rather unsociable but he has often commented to me about the great ideas that have come to his mind and the issues he has been able to resolve because of this time in his quiet place.

I, too, have utilized this same concept. Realizing the importance of time to reflect I will use a long warm shower, my driving time, my lunch breaks, a walk on a quiet trail in the mountains or park, or the time as I lay in bed getting ready to go to sleep. You, too, can find quiet, relaxing places to contemplate and emancipate the ideas imprisoned in your cluttered mind.

NUGGETS FOR THE MIND . . .

"Solitude is as needful to the imagination as society is wholesome for the character."
 --James Russell Lowell

"Solitude: A good place to visit, but a poor place to stay."
 --Josh Billings

"By all means use some time to be alone."
 --George Herbert

"Some people study all their life, and at death they have learned everything except how to think."
 --Author Unknown

"Save a space for silence in your day."
 --Author Unknown

"The heart must have its time of snow . . . to rest in silence, and then to grow."
 --Author Unknown

#23 FORGET THE PAST AND LOOK TOWARD THE FUTURE

The past can bury you, but the future gives you hope and light. I love to look forward, it is my choice. In fact, I look so much to the future that I dwell very little on the past.

Once there was a young sailor who climbed the mast to correct the sail. As he looked down he began to get sick seeing the rushing water below. An older and wiser sailor on the deck cried to him from below, "look up, look up." As the young sailor looked up toward the sky, his vision became clear and he finished his task.

When you look down, look back, or worry about the past, you lose self-confidence. You lose direction. You start going in circles and have trouble finishing even the smallest of tasks. But when you look forward, to the top of the mountain, overwhelming as it may be, you become focused, it's easier keep your eyes on the goal.

Do this and you will not be diverted by all the side roads clamoring to distract you on your journey. Your vision will be clear and you will find excitement in the new and bright prospects awaiting you.

Let the poets look to the dreary past and write poetry of doom. You write of fulfillment and success as you look toward the future and see the great hopes that tomorrow has in store.

NUGGETS FOR THE MIND . . .

"Perhaps the best thing about the future is that it comes one day at a time."
 --Dean Acheson

"The only part of time that's of interest to me is the future. That's where I'm going to spend the rest of my life."
 --Charles F. Kettering

"I never think about the past, only about the present and the future, and I always conceive of myself as growing. I have never had one second of boredom since I was born."
 --Mary Martin

"The past cannot be changed; the future is still in your power."
 --Author Unknown

"I like the dreams of the future better than the history of the past."
 --Thomas Jefferson

"Think to yourself that every day is your last; the hour to which you do not look forward will come as a welcome surprise. As for me, when you want a good laugh, you will find me, in a fine state, fat and sleek, a true hog of Epicurus' herd."
 --Horace [Quintas Horatius Flaccus]

" You cannot undo the past, but the past can undo you!"
 -- Sam Spencer

#24   CARRY A SPARE TIRE

Whenever you travel in your automobile, you certainly carry a spare tire. When was the last time you used it? If you are like me, it has been a long time. Yet you still carry one. Why? This keeps you prepared for the little mishaps that show up from time to time. Maybe you need to carry special medication with you, an extra copy of your proposal or presentation, or some other need. The scout motto is "Be Prepared." That says it all!

Recently I went on a fishing trip. We had used my fish finder to locate the fish. We could find no fish in the lake at all. We kept trolling about 20 feet deep and after a couple of hours we finally gave up. We went over to our friends and learned that they had caught several fish right next to the shore in only about five feet of water. We could not fish the shallow water because we had only brought equipment to fish in the deeper water. The fish finder was showing more fish along the shore, but we didn't have a "spare tire" fit for the occasion.

What are the spare tires you should carry? Maybe it's extra money in the bank, enough food to last a few weeks, another pair of glasses, more education, other skills, etc. Go to your quiet place and ponder this question – "What are the spare tires that I should be carrying?" (And by the way, be certain that your car's spare tire is filled with air.)

NUGGETS FOR THE MIND . . .

"It is thrifty to prepare today for the wants of tomorrow."
 --Aesop

"The door of opportunity is wide open if you are prepared."
 --Author Unknown

"A man who qualifies himself well for his calling, never fails of employment."
 --Thomas Jefferson

> Keep a poem in you pocket
> And a picture in your head
> And you'll never feel lonely
> At night when you're in bed.
>
> The little poem will sing to you
> Thoughts the picture will bring to you
> And you'll never feel lonely
> At night when you're in bed.
> 						Beatrice de Regniers

"Success depends upon previous preparation, and without such preparation there is sure to be failure."
 --Confucius

#25 THINK OF YOUR TANK AS HALF FULL

This relates to the way you think. Half full is a bit more positive than half empty. They both describe the same exact situation, however, when you say them both aloud you will see which one makes you feel more positive. The phrases that make you feel better will also make others feel better. The way you speak, the words you use, the tone of your voice, all dictate attitude, and your attitude effects all others around you.

There are many phrases you use that can be said either in a positive or a negative manner. Think of a positive way to phrase it. Ask yourself each day, "How can I look at this issue as if the tank were half full?" Look at it as an opportunity for success rather than some previous failure.

Your mind is a very powerful tool. You can even hasten the healing of some illnesses by thinking that you are getting well and visualizing the end result. Make it a habit to think of positive, uplifting phraseology in all your conversations, even with negative situations.

Here are some example phrases:

...Rather than - You are always late. Use - You seldom arrive on time.
...Rather than - You work too slow. Use - You can work faster, I've seen you!

Negative language creates negative feelings. Positive language creates trust, empowers, and builds. Which traits would like to foster?

NUGGETS FOR THE MIND . . .

"For myself I am an optimist -- it does not seem to be much use being anything else."
--Prime Minister Winston Churchill

"Keep your face to the sunshine and you cannot see the shadow."
--Helen Keller

"Let us not go over the old ground, let us rather prepare for what is to come."
--Marcus Tullius Cicero

"The only difference between a rut and a grave is that one is just a little deeper than the other."
--Author Unknown

"No one can ever overcome anything until his thoughts are creative and positive."
--Norman Vincent Peale

"It is often difficult to change circumstances, but a positive attitude can help lift discouragement."
--Val R. Christensen

"Every exit is an entry somewhere else."
--Tom Stoppard

#26 WATCH YOURSELF PERFORM YOUR TASK

On occasion you may perform poorly, and if you could see yourself, you probably would say, "I don't believe I did that." Stop, back-up and think about how you acted and maybe next time you will think about it differently. Often I have said to myself, "Maybe I should have spoken less, maybe I shouldn't have moved so quickly or spoken so fast." As you do this, you notice the things you need to do to polish your skills for greater success. Stop and take a look at how you do what you do.

Maybe you're out of control. At times the basketball player will drive down the middle of the court a little faster than his ability allows. The coach lets him watch the tapes of the game and tells him, "See how you were a little out of control coming down the key? Next time what you need to do is dribble that ball a little bit differently, not so fast, and you'll have the control you need."

You need to do the same with your life, just as the professional sports person is trying to develop the most perfect skill he can, you should do the same. Be your own coach. Take some time each day to review your performance and allow yourself opportunity to develop. To do this more effectively you will have to become more aware of your mannerisms and style.

An important key to improvement is recognizing where improvement is needed through observation. It works the same for "self" – For self-improvement, recognizing your needs come from self-observation.

NUGGETS FOR YOUR MIND . . .

"The way we imagine ourselves to appear to another person is an essential element in conception of ourselves. In other words, I am not what I think I am, and I am not what you think I am. I am what I think you think I am."
 --Robert Bierstedt

"You will always have to live with yourself, and it is to your best interest to see that you have good company -- a clean, pure, straight, honest, upright, generous, magnanimous companion."
 --Orison Swett Marden

"The reward for being true to a correct principle is worth whatever it costs, and often the greatest reward is the character development in the person who remains true."
 --Author Unknown

"You miss 100 percent of the shots you never take."
 --Wayne Gretsky

"To know oneself is to study oneself in action with another person."
 --Bruce Lee

A SMALL PRICE
Pay attention to what you do and say,
That is the cheapest price to pay.
So when time and space have gone their way,
You won't be taunted by that day.
 --Sam Spencer

#27 LISTEN TO YOURSELF SPEAK TO OTHERS

My wife commented to me that when she was growing up her mother would say to her, "I wish you could hear how you talk to your brothers. I just wish I had a tape recorder." You know what I mean! If you heard yourself speak to others, would you speak differently?

Try this. After you have been talking to someone, pause and think of not only what you said, but how you said it. I recall the phrase, "the tone makes the music." Don't be so stuck on your authority or position that you eliminate kindness as you talk to others.

Sometimes you see the problem too late. My brother and I were in a store completing a purchase. We were in a hurry. My mind was preoccupied with our project and the need to get back. I got my change from the cashier and hurried to the car. As we drove off, my brother commented, "You sure were short with that young sales lady." I hadn't noticed. Generally I try to be just the opposite because as a young man I had often been in her situation. As I thought back over the sequence of events, he was right. We were long gone by now. I couldn't have gone back, I could only be even kinder to the next person.

The words you say and the way you say them will be a good indication of the kind of person you are. Listen to what you say! Make sure you are conveying the message you truly want to convey. Make sure your speech is consistent with who you are and who you want to be.

NUGGETS FOR THE MIND . . .

"Resolve to know thyself and know he that finds himself loses his misery."
--Author Unknown

"Never be sparing with words of appreciation, especially when they are deserved by those around us. Everyone likes to be told that they are admired, respected, appreciated, and even liked"
--Author Unknown

"Always be nice to people on the way up; because you'll meet the same people on the way down."
--Wilson Mizner

"Where there is love there is hope."
--David L. Cardinalli

"Build bridges instead of walls and you will have a friend."
--Author Unknown

"It usually takes more than three weeks to prepare a good impromptu speech. "
--Mark Twain

"Doubt yourself and you doubt everything you see. Judge yourself and you see judges everywhere. But if you listen to the sound of your own voice, you can rise above doubt and judgment. And you can see forever."
--Nancy Kerrigan

#28 KNOW WHEN TO BACK UP

In the pursuit of your goals you sometimes find yourself stuck in what seems to be a dead end or you may be going in circles. Step back, study it again. You might need to back-up!

When I was 18, my friend and I were hunting rabbits in the desert. We were driving an old station wagon that I am sure my father let us use because he remembered being a boy once, too. We would get stuck in the sand and then dig and push our way out. On this occasion we were stuck in the wash below the road working our way back to the road. We would line the path of the wheels with branches and one of us pushed while the other drove. We struggled for over an hour.

Finally after much effort we were only within five feet of the road. The going was very difficult and slow. Just then two cowboys, hats, boots and pick-up truck, from New Mexico State University drove up and asked if we needed help. Excitedly, we invited them to assist us. I had a quick vision of them pulling out a chain or rope and pulling us out. One fellow climbed into the driver's seat of our car, threw it into reverse, and backed down to the bottom again. Before I had time to yell and get angry he gunned the motor, threw it into drive and with new momentum, picked a new path and shot through the sand up to the road.

How many times have you lost your momentum, and you are stuck, inching along doing the same old thing. Stop! Look the situation over, back-up and get increased momentum, perhaps choose a new direction, but don't give up on your goal.

NUGGETS FOR THE MIND . . .

"When ever I arrive at a dead end, I back up and try a new road."
--Sam Spencer

"If at first you don't succeed, start over!"
--Author Unknown

"Happiness is not a reward--it is a consequence. Suffering is not a punishment-- it is a result."
--Robert Green Ingersoll

"When you reach a turning point in life--TURN"
--Sam Spencer

"When you get into a tight place and everything goes against you, till it seems as though you could not hold on a minute longer, never give up then, for that is just the place and time that the tide will turn."
--Harriet Beecher Stowe

"Continue to do the same old thing, and you'll continue to end up at the same old place. You'll never do better! And finally, one morning, you'll wake up, and find, you're out of the race!"
--Sam Spencer

#29   CONTROL YOUR ENVIRONMENT

You are a product of your environment. You may not realize how much you actually can control your environment. I walk into various places of business and see the little cubicles six feet by six feet and a six foot high wall to divide the officettes. Everyone is in the same common area with all these cubical offices. I think "How can you work with all these people?" The key is controlling your environment. I see some who have flowers on their desks, pictures of their family, posters, light-hearted calendars and a real homey environment. They may not be able to control all their environment, but they can control enough that they can enjoy work.

Your environment includes those with whom you associate. You may find that the language and actions of your associates are in conflict with your principles. If you remain in such a situation, you must be on guard against falling into the pattern of behavior of your peers and associates and becoming like them.

Consider controlling your "people" environment by being selective in choosing your associates. Cultivate intimate friendships with those whose lives you wish to emulate. This is not to say that you never associate with people who don't have the same goals and values you have. Recognize that you are influenced greatly by your environment. Look at the schools, look at your work. Most people fall into the trap of beginning to act and talk like everyone else. Don't be content to be a "carbon copy."

NUGGETS FOR THE MIND...

"The environment fosters and selects; the seed must contain the potentiality and direction of the life to be selected."
 --George Santayana

"Never before has man had such capacity to control his own environment, to end thirst and hunger, to conquer poverty and disease, to banish illiteracy and massive human misery. We have the power to make this the best generation of mankind in the history of the world -- or to make it the last."
 --President John F. Kennedy

"Cursed is he that does not know when to shut his mind. An open mind is all very well in its way, but it ought not to be so open that there is no keeping anything in or out of it. It should be capable of shutting its doors sometimes, or may be found a little draughty."
 --Samuel Butler

"Your future is not determined by circumstances over which you have no control, but is conditioned by the attitude you have toward yourself, toward other people, toward the world, and toward God."
 --Norman Vincent Peale

"I do not believe in a fate that falls on all men however they act: but I do believe in a fate that falls on them unless they act."
 --G.K. Chesterton

#30   SHAKE HANDS FIRMLY - LOOK THE OTHER PERSON IN THE EYE

How do you like the dead fish hand shake? Maybe you have one! If you do, trade it in on a new hardy, firm model! A firm hand shake and eye-to-eye contact denotes self-confidence, a good attitude, enthusiasm and a happy spirit.

Your body language sends an important message. Grasp the other person's hand firmly, shake it. Look him straight in the eyes and ask him something about himself. You will make a great impression. Your first impression may stay with another a long time so remember you have only one opportunity to make that first impression. If this is a quick interview, every little detail will be important. A firm hand shake could easily make the difference. Make this a habit today so when you need to rely on a firm hand shake it is as natural to you as walking.

It is interesting, once you embrace this nugget, to see how many people look away as you look then in the eyes. You will notice a big difference in the level of success
Analyze every hand shake others give you. Choose a few of those hand shakes that make you feel good. Study them and make yours a combination of the ones you prefer. Remember, if you like it, others will too.

NUGGETS FOR THE MIND . . .

"Confidence is contagious. So is lack of confidence"
--Vince Lombardi

"Enthusiasm is the producer of confidence that cries to the world, 'I've got what it takes' without uttering a word to boast."
--Paul J. Meyer

"Success or failure depends more upon attitude than upon capacity...successful men act as though they have accomplished or are enjoying something. Soon it becomes a reality. Act, look, feel successful, conduct yourself accordingly, and you will be amazed at the positive results."
--Dr. DuPree Jordan, Jr.

"If you have no confidence in self, you are twice defeated in the race of life. With confidence, you have won even before you have started."
--Marcus Garvey

"Act as though it is im to fail."
--Author Unknown

"I was always looking outside myself for strength and confidence but it comes from within."
--Author Unknown

#31 ONLY JUDGE YOURSELF AGAINST YOURSELF

Each one of us gleans differently from our life's experiences. Even though you may walk the exact same path, each person has his own interpretation of that experience. Many have experienced the exact same event you have perhaps at a different time in life or from a different vantage point. Consequently, no experience will or can ever be exactly the same for any two people.

You must learn to judge yourself only against yourself. At times this is difficult to do. Here are some steps that help:

...Write in a journal where you feel you are today.
...One week from today analyze yourself and write down in your journal where you are at that time.
...Recognize and acknowledge your progress.
...Continue to do this at appropriate intervals.
...Chart and record to appreciate YOUR growth.

Good businesses, while aware of the competition, are always competing against themselves. My father would show me his graphs of past business performance as he compared them to his current figures. He was constantly aware of where he had been and knew where he was going.

As you compete against yourself you must also be aware of your limitations. Being aware of your limitations will help you realize what you need to work on to improve or when to just stop. The key is being honest with yourself; take full responsibility for both your words and your actions, then, do your best. You will always be pleased if are doing is your best.

NUGGETS FOR THE MIND . . .

"We judge ourselves by what we feel capable of doing, while others judge us by what we have already done."
 --Henry Wadsworth Longfellow

"Judge a man by what he finishes, not by what he begins."
 --Author Unknown

"Even God doesn't plan to judge a man til the end of his days, why should you and I."
 --Author Unknown

"Before I judge my neighbor, let me walk a mile in his moccasins."
 --Sioux Proverb

"The charges we bring against others often come home to ourselves; we inveigh against faults which are as much ours as theirs; and so eloquence ends by telling against ourselves."
 --St. Jerome

"If we could first know where we are, and whither we are tending, we could then better judge what to do, and how to do it."
 --Abraham Lincoln

"I have no faults, just imperfect character traits."
 --Author Unknown

#32   ADVERSITY IS THE BEST WAY TO GROW

I appreciate adversity, not because of it's anxious moments, but because I have learned over the years that when I have those difficult moments I become stronger and grow in many ways. It's never fun at the time, but when you see how it helped you grow, or how it helped you change for the better, the experience becomes valuable. Adversity is only a challenge, or a snag in your life. Recognize that adversities are life's stepping stones.

Examine a weight lifter for example. As he lifts weights it is the resistance against his muscles that builds his strength. It is the number of repetitions that gives him his stamina. The greater the resistance, the more strength he builds, the greater the number of repetitions the more stamina he builds.

It is the same with you. As you face and conquer adversity you build stamina. You become victorious in your challenge. You build sufficient strength to move the obstacles which impede your progress. As you confront adversity and endure it's challenges you grow in vital ways: acceptance of life, recognition of self, persistence, knowledge, and understanding, to mention only a few.

As you study great people you will find that many overcame great adversity in their lives. It was the process of overcoming that established the life long traits that led to their success. Recognize adversity as a stepping stone to bigger and better things.

NUGGETS FOR THE MIND . . .

"By trying we can easily learn to endure adversity -- another man's."
--Mark Twain

"He that has never known adversity, is but half acquainted with others, or with himself. Constant success shows us but one side of the world; for as it surrounds us with friends, who tell us only merits, so it silences those enemies from whom only we can learn defects."
--Colton

"If you are too fortunate, you will not know yourself. If you are too unfortunate, nobody will know you."
--Thomas Fuller

"if all our misfortunes were laid in one common heap whence everyone must take an equal portion, most people would be contented to take their own and depart."
--Socrates

"Adversity is the trial of principal. Without it a man hardly knows whether hi is honest or not."
--Henry Fielding

"SUCCESS: A plan is a trap laid to capture the future."
--Louis A. Allen

#33 HAVE A MENTOR - IDOL - SOMEONE YOU CAN LEARN FROM

What is a mentor? A mentor is a trusted advisor, tutor or coach, someone you can go to for direction, advice and answers. This is generally an individual who has traveled the path you are traveling.

When I started my wooden toy manufacturing business, I was not a woodworker. I had developed several wooden products and began selling them to retail stores. I found that I needed some advice. I became acquainted with a person who is now a good friend, who was very helpful. On many occasions I would go to his business seeking advice about a particular procedure or where to obtain special raw material. At various markets I attended I would always ask others about their procedures in their business. When you find out what others have accomplished, you also load your arsenal with their experiences. You may not need these new ideas now, but you can file them away for later use. Remember, you never go fishing with only one hook. Have several ideas stored away for a later date.

You must have enough courage to ask for help and advice from others more experienced. One of the greatest obstacles in learning is not being able to accept the facts that you don't have all the answers. Analyze the information you receive from your mentors, then use what you feel fits your needs, personality, and current situation. How do you find a mentor? You talk to every qualified person that you can and to those who respond, ask them all the questions they will answer. Study and apply the appropriate answers. Give them thanks and the credit they deserve along the way.

NUGGETS FOR THE MIND . . .

"Others will follow your footsteps easier than they will your advice."
 --Author Unknown

"I bid him look into the lives of men as though into a mirror, and from others to take an example for himself."
 --Terence [Publius Terentius Afer]

"The scars of others should teach us caution."
 --St. Jerome

"The first great gift we can bestow on others is a good example."
 --Morell

"He that won't be counselled can't be helped."
 --Ben Franklin

"No man is so foolish but he may sometimes give another good counsel, and no man so wise that he may not easily err if he takes no other counsel than his own. He that is taught only by himself has a fool for a master"
 --Ben Johnson

#34   KEEP YOUR LIFE SIMPLE

Albert Einstein said, "Everything should be made as simple as , but not simpler." Life can get to be so hectic, become frustrating with going here and going there, doing this and doing that! Trying to please everyone will leave you lost and forgotten along the way. Find ways to simplify your life by asking yourself a few questions as you go through your day. Here are some suggested questions that will help:

...How essential is what I am doing?
...Who does it make happy?
...Who will benefit from....(task)?
...Will this take me closer to my long-term goals?
...What do I have that I don't need any more?
...Do I really need to go this fast?

The answers to these questions will help give you direction. You will be able to see more clearly the areas that you can delete.

Eliminate the clutter and simplify. If you have junk in your garage, junk in your desk at work, junk in your daily activities, or junk in your speech, simplify! Have a mental garage sale. Clean house of all the projects that don't have any purpose any more. Where , eliminate those things from your life that no longer make you happy or gratify you. Quit spending time on dead ends taking you no place. Simplify your life! Simplify! Simplify! Simplify!

NUGGETS FOR THE MIND . . .

"Nothing is more simple than greatness; indeed, to be simple is to be great."
  --Ralph Waldo Emerson

"Observe due measure, for right timing is in all things the most important factor."
  --Hesiod

"You cannot see the wood for the trees."
  --John Heywood

"The great artist is the simplifier."
  --Henri Frederic Amiel

"Our life is frittered away by detail. Simplicity, simplicity, simplicity!"
  -- Henry David Thoreau

"Simplicity is making the journey through life with just enough baggage."
  --Charles Dudley Warner

#35 CREATE GOOD HABITS TO REPLACE BAD HABITS

You are always talking about establishing good habits. Why not look over your bad ones and say, "Good-bye bad habit, I'm going to replace you with this good one." By concentrating on a new good habit, you are focusing a positive effort on acquiring something you want rather than negative energy on something that bothers you. As you focus on the good, the bad will fade away.

Everyone has bad habits. In fact, you could write your own book, "My 101 Best Bad Habits." So do that! Take a piece of paper and write the bad habits you would like to get rid of in one column and then write the good habits you would like to replace them with in the other. This gives you a great place to begin. Choose the easiest ones first to help establish, in the subconscious, a pattern of success. Progressively work your way along to the most difficult ones on the list. Here are some steps that you will find helpful:

...Accept the habit as something you want to change.
...Outline the steps you will take to replace the old habit.
...Put reminders up at home, at work, and in the car.
...Let close friends know what you are doing and ask for help.

Remember that you alone have the power to change yourself and that all real change comes from within. Therefore you must have ample desire to motivate you to action. As you practice this replacement technique you will get better and better. Soon you will find self-improvement to be exciting and greatly rewarding.

NUGGETS FOR THE MIND...

"We first make habits, and then habits break us."
--John Dryden

"Whatever you would make habitual, practice it; and if you would not make a thing habitual, do not practice it, but accustom yourself to something else."
--Epictetus

"It is easy to assume a habit; but when you try to cast it off, it will take skin and all."
--Henry Wheeler Shaw

"The second half of a man's life is made up of nothing but the habits he has acquired during the first half."
--Feodor Dostoevski

> Sow an act and you reap a habit.
> Sow a habit and you reap a character.
> Sow a character and you reap a destiny.
> --Charles Reade

"A habit cannot be tossed out the window; it must be coaxed down the stairs a step at a time."
--Mark Twain

#36 ANALYZE THE NEXT STEP

This idea will keep you aware of both where you are now and where you want to be. I don't mean such routine tasks as; now it's time to go to work, or now it's time to eat lunch. I mean what is the next step in your career, in your life, with your family, or in your goals. These are direction questions to help you stay on course through your life's journey.

Your next step may be to start a part-time business, to get additional education, to correct some personal habits or, perhaps, to take some time out to rest and rejuvenate. Life is a series of phases or steps. Good definition maintains focus and direction.

After I sold my last business I needed time to rest. I needed time to think and gain a renewed perspective. Time to look at different opportunities and find a new direction. I was once again in a position to start another new and exciting journey. I just wanted to be sure that I was heading in the direction that I wanted to go.

Ask yourself, "Where am I today?" "Where do I want to be tomorrow?" "How do I plan to get where I want to be?" "What is the next step I need to take to get there?" "Who can help me along the way?" "What are the attitudes or the obstacles preventing me from going forward?"

I enjoy hiking the Rocky Mountains. I must always look ahead to find the best path to follow. So, too, with your life, keep focused in the direction you wish to go and you will find the next trail you should follow. When you reach the next trail, you can continue without hesitation.

NUGGETS FOR THE MIND . . .

"The man who has no goal who doesn't know where he's going, and whose thoughts must therefore be thoughts of confusion and anxiety and fear and worry...becomes what he thinks about."
 --Earl Nightingale

"Adversity reveals genius, prosperity conceals it."
 --Horace

"So many new ideas are at first strange and horrible though ultimately valuable that a very heavy responsibility rests upon those who would prevent their dissemination."
 --J.B.S. Haldane

"As dogs in a wheel, or squirrels in a cage, ambitious men still climb and climb, with great labor and incessant anxiety, but never reach the top."
 --Burton

"Success comes one step at a time, not giant steps, but lots of little steps."
 --Sam Spencer

#37 STOP SAYING "I CAN'T" AND START SAYING "HOW CAN I?"

What's this "I can't?" "Who taught you that?" Withdraw from that type of person. He will do you little good. I am extremely uncomfortable around negative people. They are like a cancer. In any group they begin to find fault, tear down and ruin a good progressive spirit.

Several years ago I went into a bank to borrow $2,500 to start a new business. I offered my car which had a value of at least two times the loan requested. The banker laughed at me and said my idea wouldn't work and when I failed they would have nothing but a bad note and a pile of sticks. He wasn't even polite. Ten years later I sold the business that the apprehensive banker said would never succeed, and at a fair profit, I might add.

I didn't give up; I looked at the "how can I?" answers to my problems and pursued them until I achieved the desired success. You can do the same. Look for the "how can I?" solution every time you hear some self-made failure tell you that you can't. Expand your options by talking to others. There will be those who are the "you can't" people, pay no attention to them. Replace them with "you can" people and keep talking to this constructive group of people.

You must be the first one to ask yourself this question, "How Can I?" Make this a new habit and you will be unstoppable. Become your own "self-made" success story by always asking yourself -- "How can I?"

NUGGETS FOR THE MIND . . .

POSITIVE ATTITUDE
If you think you are beaten, you are.
If you think you dare, you don't.
If you'd like to win but think you can't,
It's almost a cinch you won't.
Life's battles don't always go
To the stronger or faster man.
But soon or late the man who wins
Is the one who thinks he can.
--Author Unknown

"Ah, but a man's reach should exceed his grasp, or what's a heaven for?"
--Robert Browning

"An obstacle is something you see when you take your eyes off the goals you are trying to reach."
--Author Unknown

"If you will tell me why the fen appears impassable,
I then will tell you why
I think that I can cross it if I try."
--Marianne Moore

"The world is moving so fast these days that the man who says it can't be done is generally interrupted by someone doing it."
--Elbert Hubbart

#38 THINK YOUR PROJECT THROUGH AND ACT IT OUT

An actor will read the script, think through the part and then act it out. A professional athlete will prepare a game plan and then practice or "act out" his plan for victory. This process leads to each individual's success. Adopt the same process in your life. Take sufficient time to mentally rehearse and go through the actions.

It works in any project. For a job interview rehearsal, sit in a chair and respond aloud to questions you may be asked. For meeting an important person, stand in front of the mirror and practice what you might say. This will take some of the fear and anxiety away.

When I prepare a new speech I go to my quiet place. I stand and give the speech with the emotion and movement that I intend to present before my audience. When I designed a new product, I would go through the manufacturing process to see what I might have missed. Then I would go over to the machinery and without turning on a machine I would act out each process to be sure it worked mechanically before I took the hours necessary to prepare prototypes. I could see changes I needed to make before I dedicated time and material for production.

Each time you start something new, each time you plan to meet a new person, each time you are ready to learn a new procedure, take time to think through the process and then act it out. As you do this you get valuable information that can help you to foresee and correct any potential problem.

NUGGETS FOR THE MIND . . .

> Four things a man must learn to do
> If he would make his record true:
> To think, without confusion, clearly;
> To act, from honest motives, purely;
> To love his fellow men sincerely,
> To trust in God and heaven securely.
> --Henry Van Dyke

"Think then act safely."
--Author Unknown

> You are the person who has to decide
> Whether you'll do it or toss it aside;
> You are the person who makes up your mind
> Whether you'll lead or will linger behind --
> Whether you'll try for the goal that's afar
> Or just be contented to stay where you are."

Edgar A. Guest

"The Lord gave us two ends to use. One to think with and one to sit with. The war depends on which one we use, heads we win, tails we lose."
--Author Unknown

"The discovery of what is true and the practice of that which is good, are the two most important aims of philosophy."
--Voltaire

#39   ACT, DON'T RE-ACT

STOP! LOOK! THINK! Take time to think before you act. Then your actions will be made with the best interest of all in mind. Over reacting to any particular situation can hurt feelings and cause irreparable damage. Know the facts well enough that your actions will be well founded.

I had a young man work for me who had trouble listening to directions and staying on task. However, I felt a desire to try to help him. I would give him one assignment at a time to be sure he made no mistakes. One day I had him prepare a stack of doll high chair sides for drilling. I emphasized that he was not to drill them until I reviewed the process with him. Upon completion he was to inform me and I would instruct him on the next task. After some time I returned to his work station to see why he was taking so long. There he was drilling each one wrong. I saw $500 worth of product lost in just minutes.

Iquestions I invited him to get a broom and sweep the floors while I collected my thoughts. To yell and scream would do him no good. To let the matter go would do me no good. I went to my office to think it through and to arrive at the best solution. After I collected my thoughts, he and I had a meeting about the problem and reached a compatible and reasonable solution.

Take time to review and think before you act, you can never recall your actions or your words. Carefully planned actions will lead to fewer apologies and regrets.

NUGGETS FOR THE MIND . . .

"Think twice before you speak, then say it to yourself first."
--Author Unknown

"When anger rises, think of the consequences."
--Confucious

"Don't go off half-cocked --- Take time to be sure you are fully-cocked"
--Sam Spencer

"Next to temperance, a quiet conscience, a cheerful mind and active habits, I place early rising as a means of health and happiness."
--Timothy Flint

"Since the creation of the world there has been no tyrant like Intemperance, and no slaves so cruelly treated as his."
--William Lloyd Garrison

"The best time to hold your tongue is the time you feel you must say something or bust."
--Josh Billings

#40   ALWAYS BE WILLING TO LEARN

From the very first breath you breathe you begin to learn. There are only two things you can control about your learning. One is how you will learn. You may choose to learn slowly or you may choose to learn quickly, but you will learn! The second is what you do with what you learn. You may allow your knowledge to lay dormant, you may act on it immediately or something in between. However, how you learn and what you do with your knowledge will affect you enormously!

There is so much to learn in so many different areas. If you ever decide you have no more need to learn you are in big trouble. Learn to invest in yourself, store something away for tomorrow. When you gain new knowledge, things change inside. It may be a weakness pointed out by a friend, a broader perspective of life, or a new theory at work. When you learn, your understanding increases, and because you understand, you become willing to change or act on that knowledge.

Think of learning as conquering a new mountain, each step is a small progression in the right direction, with each bit of knowledge you obtain. Learning takes you to new horizons, brings new happiness into your life, it opens new doors, gives you greater awareness, and teaches you what you must do. To keep up in this ever changing world you must constantly be seeking new knowledge. Ask yourself, "Am I willing to learn?" "Am I teachable?" If you have trouble answering yes to these questions, then ask yourself, "How can I become willing?" A willingness to learn is vital to any success.

NUGGETS FOR THE MIND . . .

"Do not think that what your thoughts dwell upon is of no matter. Your thoughts are making you."
 --Bishop Steere

"Knowledge is essential to conquest, only according to ignorance are we helpless."
 --Annie Bessant

"The universe is full of magical things just waiting for wits to grow sharper."
 --Author Unknown

"Those who do not read are no better off than those who cannot read."
 --Author Unknown

"Man is the only one that knows nothing, that can learn nothing without being taught. He can neither speak nor walk nor eat, and in short he can do nothing at the prompting of nature only, but weep."
 --Pliny the Elder

"The person who says he is too old to learn was probably always too old."
 --Author Unknown

#41   REALIZE THAT OTHERS DON'T HAVE THE SAME PERSPECTIVE YOU DO

You are the sum total of all your learning and experiences. No two people are exactly alike. My twin daughters have two distinct ideas and opinions. Their interests, while sometimes the same, vary greatly, both in intensity as well as perception. When you understand that each person's perspective is different from yours, especially in things that are emotional by nature, your acceptance of them will become broader and more complete. You will begin to understand why they are where they are, what they have become, and why they say what they say.

Sometimes I've hired a new person to work at a particular station in the assembly line. To help them get the same perspective I had, we would go to the show room and look at the completed product assembled and in use. They would grasp a picture of what they were making. When I did this they would make fewer mistakes and the workmanship would be better. Once they "got the picture," my job was easier, and so was theirs.

Remember when you saw something unique in the distance, like a rock formation or a cloud picture? You might have invited others to share the view. It had to be seen from your exact vantage point to get the full impact. You moved them around, twisted their heads and even tried to line up their sights to make out the far-off formation. Some were able to see it, others did not. Some saw it but didn't grasp the image. Life is like that too, you try to help people get the same perspective you have. Some will, some won't. Many times both are right, but with different interpretations.

NUGGETS FOR THE MIND...

"The view-points of others are like snowflakes; there are millions of them, and no two are alike."
  --Sam Spencer

"Respecting differences means giving freedom to think, and considering their views as deeply as your own."
  --Steven R, Covey

"Words differently arranged have a different meaning, and meanings differently arranged have a different effect."
  --Blaise

"The main distinction between you and your friend is that you both are different."
  --Sam Spencer

"The key to valuing those differences is to realize that all people see the world, not as it is, but as they are."
  --Steven R. Covey

"We all live under the same sky but we don't have the same horizon."
  --Author Unknown

#42 PLAN AND PRACTICE YOUR RESPONSE SKILLS

One of the most difficult tasks you will ever encounter is being interviewed by others or meeting someone for the first time. Equal to this is being confronted with an unusual situation or question. Although this can be frightening, there are some steps you can take to prepare yourself. It has been said, "If you are prepared you shall not fear."

Here are some steps you can take to better prepare yourself for the inevitable unexpected:

...Practice shaking hands and greeting others.
...Write down all the conceivable questions one might ask you.
...Practice answering your questions in the mirror or to a friend.
...Arrive at your appointment early enough to become comfortable with the surroundings.
...Envision what you are about to pursue.
...Don't second guess, but imagine responses.

When a boxer prepares to meet his opponent in the ring, he practices those skills which will be best suited to gain victory. He will focus on the event to become as well prepared as he possibly can. Through planning, practice and imagining the situation, you too can help yourself prepare to act with poise and confidence.

Practice this idea and you will have fewer surprises. You will be better prepared for new daily challenges. Personal confidence will grow and you will welcome new and difficult challenges.

NUGGETS FOR THE MIND . . .

"Try to put into practice what you already know, and in so doing you will in good time discover the hidden things which you now inquire about."
 --Henry Van Dyke

"Confidence and courage come through preparation and practice."
 --Author Unknown

"Practice yourself, for heaven's sake, in little things; and thence proceed to greater."
 --Epictetus

"The more tools you take with you on your journey through life the better chance you will have to get things going again after things break down."
 --Sam Spencer

"No one would ever have crossed the ocean if he could have gotten off the ship in a storm."
 --Charles F. Kettering

"When I was little, my grandfather used to make me stand in a closet for five minutes without moving.
He said it was elevator practice."
 --Steve Wright

#43   LEARN TO GOVERN YOURSELF

You must learn to govern yourself. When you come into this world many decisions are made for you. This is okay until you approach adulthood when you must now accept responsibility for your decisions. It is essential to learn to govern your own life sensibly. Life can be one of chaos, without order, loud and full of debris. You can make life a peaceful, efficient, and positive place to experience daily events.

A good king will make rules for his subjects. These rules will be applicable to their needs. He will implement programs to help them accomplish their goals. He will take the lead, especially in difficult tasks. If his subjects get out of line, he will discipline them swiftly and appropriately. This you must do if you are to be the monarch of your personal empire.

Envision yourself as the king over the "Kingdom Of Myself." How you govern yourself will determine the kingdom over which you will reign. Rule your kingdom as you would expect an honorable ruler to reign. Be fair and honest with yourself, and don't allow yourself any special privileges. Remember, you are building character in your subject *you*. Character is nothing more than what you do when there is no one around to watch. Establish your guidelines, your rules, your values, and your parameters; then govern yourself well. You must always be honest and fair. Never deceive yourself, at times this seems the easy way out but it will destroy what you have built. Become an excellent monarch!

NUGGETS FOR THE MIND . . .

"Govern thyself then you will be able to govern the world."
--Author Unknown

"Conquer thyself. Till thou hast done that; thou art a slave; for it is almost as well to be in subjection to another's appetite as thine own."
--Burton

"People are always making rules for themselves and always finding loopholes."
--Author Unknown

"The real acid test of courage is to be just your honest self when everybody is trying to be like somebody else."
--Andrew Jensen

"If one conquers a thousand men in battle, and if one conquers himself alone, he is in a battle supreme."
--Suttapitaka

"Know yourself, master yourself, conquest of self is most gratifying."
--Author Unknown

#44 IF YOU CANNOT DEPEND UPON YOURSELF, CAN OTHERS?

Dependability is one of the most important traits a person can develop. "To thine own self be true" has been said many times. So what is dependability? Being on time, showing up to work ready to work, being there when a friend needs you, supporting a good cause, not giving some lame excuse, keeping a confidence and many other small but important things.

Now ask yourself, "How dependable am I"? Don't confuse dependable with predictable. I had a young employee whom I could predict would be five or more minutes late every day. I could also predict that at least once each week Rick, without prior notice, would have to leave early for some reason. I could predict what he would do, but I could not count on him to be dependable.

I had another employee who was always to work on time. If Kevan was going to be even a few minutes late he would call and notify me. He still would do his best to make it on time, and usually he did. When he left work I knew that his work was done, that the tools were put away properly and that his area was clean. Now that's dependability! I eventually gave him the charge over the entire facility - he had earned that standing.

Become a person of whom it will be said of, "You can count on him." Dependable is not only doing what you say you will do, it is also doing what is expected of you. Dependability alone will pave the way for a happy, successful life. Dependability ranks among the greatest of all traits.

NUGGETS FOR THE MIND . . .

"What we do upon some great occasion will probably depend on what we already are; and what we will be, the result of self-discipline."
 --H. P. Liddon

"My business is not to remake myself, but to make the absolute best of what God made."
 --Robert Browning

"What other dungeon is so dark as one's own heart!"
 --Nathaniel Hawthorne

"It is difficult to make a man miserable while he feels he is worthy of himself and claims kindred to the great God who made him."
 --Abraham Lincoln

"The first and best thing is to conquer self; to be conquered by self is of all things most shameful and vile."
 --Plato

"How shall I be able to rule over others, that have not full power and command of myself?"
 --Francois Rabelais

#45 ALL CHANGE COMES FROM WITHIN

If the foundation is crumbling, the best paint job in the world won't save the house. So it is with you. To truly effect change, you must change the foundation upon which you build.

It may be necessary to make some major changes in your thinking and to change some of the negative things you do. You may say, "Very well, thank you, I like some of my negative traits." You may have held onto them all your life. No matter what anyone else says or does, until *you* decide *you* want to put forth enough effort to make the change, it will never happen. The desire must come from within. You must have a deep personal reason to change. There must be an adequate reward from this change for you personally or you will never put forth sufficient effort to succeed.

When you truly understand that all real change comes from within, you will work to build the desire to change first. Once the inner desire is strong enough, you will begin to accomplish the change both consciously and subconsciously.

Be willing to realign your foundations, change your perspective or expand your options. You might try an entirely new approach, risky, but rewarding.

Remember that another person will not change either, until he, too, has sufficient desire to change. If you want to help another work toward change then help them with the foundation and work to increase their desire to make change.

NUGGETS FOR THE MIND...

"You can never have real success 'til you meet the real person -- YOU."
 --Author Unknown

"No man is fit to command another that cannot command himself."
 --William Penn

"All that is worth cherishing on this world begins in the heart, not the head."
 --Author Unknown

"We cannot make people over. Our business is to make ourselves better and others happy, and that is a enough to keep us busy."
 --Author Unknown

"If you want to change the situation, you must first change yourself. And to change yourself effectively, you first have to change your perspective."
 --Steven R. Covey

"He that respects himself is safe from others; he wears a coat of mail that none can pierce."
 --Henry Wadsworth Longfellow

#46   REALIZE YOU ARE THE MASTER OF YOUR DESTINY

When I finally figured this out, I had no one to blame but myself for my shortcomings. I always took credit for my successes, but found it easy to place blame elsewhere for the reasons why things didn't work out the way they could have.

There are those placed in positions of influence over you. They may be positive or negative, cheerful or depressing. They may speak kindly or cruelly to you. You choose to allow either the positive or the negative to influence your life. You decide how much and in what way you will allow yourself to be affected. The choice which you make will determine the outcome in your life. So be certain your choice leads to the result you would like. The sum total of your choices in life is *you*!

Talk to yourself. Say something like this. "Will I ever see this person again?" If not, why let it bother you? He has a problem and like all the "poor me" people they only want to spread their unhappiness to others. Don't let them! Or try this: say to yourself, "I was having a real good day before he came in and now that he's leaving my day will get even better." Say it out loud, or even in a very loud voice. Sounds silly, but it really works! You try it!

When you feel like things are heading out of control, take time to ask yourself how you can regain the control. Remember that no matter what anyone says or does, they cannot control your thoughts, feelings or actions unless *you* let them. Take charge of yourself and be your own master!

NUGGETS FOR THE MIND . . .

"The more wise and powerful a master, the more directly is his work created, and the simpler it is."
--Meister Eckhart

"No one can make you feel inferior without your consent."
--Eleanor Roosevelt

"You've first got to have faith in yourself before you can do anything."
--Sterling W. Sill

"Not to have control over your senses is like sailing in a rudderless ship, bound to break to pieces on coming in contact with the very first rock."
--Mahatma Gandhi

"Know this that every soul is free, to choose his life and what he'll be."
--Unknown

"You can either be a positive or a negative in the equation of life."
--Sam Spencer

#47   STAND AND FACE YOUR PROBLEMS

Problems are an integral part of life. There are very few that will just go away if you leave them alone. You have to identify *your* problems and then face the problems. Remember that some problems are not even yours, they belong to others however you try to accept it as yours. Let them keep it! Once you learn to recognize your own problems it becomes easier to know which to leave alone and which ones to begin to solve.

The best time to solve a problem is at it's beginning. Just like the hole in the dam, the longer you wait to take care of it the bigger it will be when you finally get around to fixing it. This is not to say that you should jump on every problem instantly, but you should begin the thinking and brainstorming process.

On occasion you will need some time to think about the solutions, time to research, and time to let ideas develop. This is still facing the problem! Here are some steps to effective problem solving:

   ...Define the problem
   ...Brainstorm the solutions
   ...If , let some time pass to allow the
      subconscious to create and work
   ...Choose a workable solution
   ...Make a written plan
   ...Work the plan

On small problems you may not need to be so detailed, but you still can use most of these steps. The first and most important key to effective problem solving is to *recognize* that there *is* a problem that needs resolution.

NUGGETS FOR THE MIND . . .

"Our Problems are like dogs, stand and face them and they will run away, run away and they will chase you"
 --Hugh Nibley

"There are no big problems, there are just a lot of little problems."
 --Henry Ford

"Most problems precisely defined are already partially solved."
 --Harry Lorayne

"When you deplore the conditions in the world, ask yourself, 'Am I part of the problem or part of the solution?"
 --Author Unknown

"Probe the earth and see where your main roots run."
 --Henry David Thoreau

"If there is but little water in the stream, it is the fault, not of the channel, but of the source."
 --St. Jerome

"You gain strength, courage and confidence by every experience in which you really stop to look fear in the face. You are able to say to yourself, "I lived through this horror. I can take the next thing that comes along." . . . You must do the thing you think you cannot do."
 --Eleanor Roosevelt

#48 TAKE THE INITIATIVE - JUST DO IT!

"There is a story about four men named Everybody, Somebody, Anybody, and Nobody. There was an important job to be done, and Everybody was sure that Somebody would do it. Anybody could have done it, but Nobody did it. Somebody got angry about that, because it was Everybody's job. Everybody thought that Anybody could do it, and Nobody realized that Everybody wouldn't do it. It ended up that Everybody blamed Somebody, when actually Nobody did what Anybody could have done." (Anonymous)

This story may not be so fictitious. You may even see it from time to time in your surroundings. You possibly have been one of the characters yourself. When you see a job to be done, why not do it? What are you waiting for? Most of the time things are quite simple. This characteristic will make you feel good about yourself. My father is one who always takes the initiative. He is always fun to have around because things get done, and done right with little hesitation.

So end procrastination. Do it now! Take the initiative! Make it a goal for all this week to hop up, jump in, and do what you need to do right now. You may even get ambitious and just do all those things that have been waiting to be done. Foster this quality in your life and you will not only be well respected, but will gain many new friends and possibly be invited to participate in many worthwhile ventures.

Remember: *"Hop up, jump in, and do it now!"* The best use of your time is doing something constructive!

NUGGETS FOR THE MIND . . .

"Ours is an age which is proud of machines that think, and suspicious of any man who tries to."
--Howard Mumford Jones

"Better that we should err in action than wholly refuse to perform. The storm is so much better than the calm, as it declares the presence of a living principle. Stagnation is something worse than death. It is corruption also."
--William Gilmore Sims

"Unrest of spirit is a mark of life; one problem after another presents itself and in the solving of them we can find greatest pleasure."
--Karl Menninger

"We are very apt to measure ourselves by aspiration instead of performance. But in truth the conduct of lives is the only proof of the sincerity of hearts."
--Author Unknown

"Attempt only what you are able to perform."
--Cato

"If your ship doesn't come in, swim out to it."
--Author Unknown

#49 LOOK FOR NEW IDEAS AND NEW OPPORTUNITIES

There are new and exciting ideas being developed all the time. New packaging can often re-vitalize something old. Past overlooked opportunities and ideas may now present greater possibilities than before. One of the best ways to find success is to jump on the band wagon when it passes by. It may never come by again.

You must become creative in your thinking, not only for new ideas, but for a different application of an old one. Put several ideas together. Here is a method you can use to *brainstorm*:

...Think of as many ideas as you can.
...Do not judge any ideas until they are all out.
...List them all, good, bad, crazy, even the ridiculous.
...Keep asking; "Are there any other possibilities or approaches?"
...If , take a day or two, let the subconscious work for you.
...Go through the steps again, then begin to review.

Review:

...Categorize ideas: easiest, uniqueness, practical, etc.
...Discuss the pros and cons of each.
...Formulate a plan, then work the plan.

As you brain storm, do it creatively, with an open mind where anything goes. The mind can do amazing things, if allowed to work. Even tangents can lead to new and innovative applications. Don't forget to follow through on the last step - *Work your plan!*

NUGGETS FOR THE MIND . . .

"No one knows what he can do till he tries."
--Publilius Syrus

"Enthusiasm is the advance man who paves the way for new ideas. Maybe the enthusiasts aren't the most cultured people in the world, but they are the only ones who make history."
--Paul J. Meyer

"Ideas are like rabbits. You get a couple and learn how to handle them, and pretty soon you have a dozen."
--John Steinbeck

"A fresh mind keeps the body fresh. Take in the ideas of the day, drain off those of yesterday. As to the morrow, time enough to consider it when it becomes today."
--Edward G. Bulwer-Lytton

"Every man is the creature of the age in which he lives; very few are able to raise themselves above the ideas of the time."
--Voltaire

"A man with a new idea is a crank — until he succeeds."
--Mark Twain

#50 GAIN AND CREATE WORTHWHILE EXPERIENCES

If you think your experiences only come by chance guess again. Life presents so many opportunities of which you can take advantage. The real problem isn't that there is nothing to do, but which of all those opportunities that you could do, you will choose to do.

My wife planned a program for our family to go with two other families in our neighborhood to a nursing home and sing Christmas carols. She purposely chose a center that was hard to find, one that did not receive this type of service very often. We arrived at the center, went to the recreation area and began our little program of Christmas carols. What an experience for the children! They learned more about elderly people as they shared personal time with them before we left. One of my older daughters arranged other opportunities since that time to visit other people at rest homes accompanied by several of her friends. What a great experience my wife created for the kids (and even for dad).

What makes an experience worthwhile is the measure of growth you attain. It may be knowledge, understanding, or perspective you gain. Now that you know that you are in control of your life and the master of your destiny, be sure your experiences are worthwhile. Put yourself in situations that will provide you with opportunity to gain worthwhile experiences.

Oh and don't worry so much about what others may or may not have gained, this is *your* life, you live your life and let them live their life.

NUGGETS FOR THE MIND...

"We should be careful to get out of an experience only the wisdom that is in it -- and stop there; lest we be like the cat that sits down on a hot stove-lid. She will never sit down on a hot stove-lid again -- and that is well; but also she will never sit down on a cold one anymore."
 --Mark Twain

"All experience is an arch, to build upon."
 --Henry Adams

"Our knowledge is the amassed thought and experience of innumerable minds."
 --Ralph Waldo Emerson

"I have but one lamp by which my feet are guided, and that is the lamp of experience."
 --Patrick Henry

"No man's knowledge here can go beyond his experience."
 --John Locke

"One thing about experience is that when you don't have very much, you are apt to get a lot."
 --Author Unknown

#51   LOOK FOR THE LESSON IN YOUR LIFE'S EXPERIENCE

Every day life offers new and interesting experiences. You are writing a storybook full of adventure and excitement, happiness and sorrow. Each experience that you have is unique. No one else has ever had your exact viewpoint or perspective.

I believe that life presents lessons with regularity. It is each person's responsibility to discover the lessons and act upon them. These lessons need not be from some enormous adventure but mostly from ordinary everyday events. You can transform many of life's experiences into lessons for yourself and for others. When you use your daily experiences as a source of learning the lessons are better understood and better remembered.

Here is a simple example: Last winter I noticed our cat spending a good deal of time huddled just outside the French doors. Later I realized that she had scratched off a section of weather stripping and was seeking warmth. I recognized that a lesson could be learned from this small experience. People, just like the cat, seek warmth from others. I later used this story to teach a lesson to my young children by saying that everyone has the need to feel warm and emphasizing that each one of us should make a special point to make others feel warm from our words and our actions.

Spend some time examining the experiences of life, recognizing little opportunities to learn and improve. Ask yourself, "Is there a message for me in this?" When you use the lessons from life, often simple, but real, the message is magnified and better remembered.

NUGGETS FOR THE MIND . . .

Don't stand in your own shadow. Get your little self out of the way so your big self can stride forward.

Make the most of yourself by fanning the tiny spark of possibility within you into the flame of achievement.

Follow the advice of Socrates: "Know Thyself.", Know your strengths and your weaknesses; your relation to the universe; your potentialities; your spiritual heritage; your aims and purposes; take stock of yourself.

Create the kind of self you will be happy to live with all your life.

Consider the words of the new convert who prayed: "Oh, Lord, help me to reform the world -- beginning with me."

Be gentle with yourself, learn to love yourself, to forgive yourself, for only as we have the right attitude toward ourselves can we have the right attitude toward others.
 --Wilfred A. Peterson

"Clouds come floating into my life, no longer to carry rain or usher storm, but to add colour to my sunset sky."
 --Rabindranath Tagor Rabindranath

#52 HELP OTHERS OBTAIN THEIR GOALS

One of the most effective ways to evaluate how you are doing or who you really are is by helping others obtain their goals. This requires that you not only think of what you've accomplished, but think of how you can help others accomplish their goals.

Invariably, everyone benefits by acts of kindness. I feel there are two general ways you can help others in their personal quests. First, an opportunity is provided for you as others approach you seeking direction with a problem. Take time to share your ideas both successful and unsuccessful. Don't put pressure on them to do things your way, they must learn for themselves. Please, remember there are many avenues to achieve the same results. Respect their choices as they would yours.

The second way is the most charitable. This is when you are aware of another person's struggle to reach a goal, or you see someone performing a difficult task, you then take time to assist. Maybe you feel like I do, just having someone to assist when having a difficult task to do somehow made it much more pleasant.

One evening I was laying sod in my large yard. Soon several neighbors offered to assist. "Of course," I said. Swiftly, the new assistants helped me with my task. I was extremely appreciative and because of their unexpected kindness I was motivated to work even harder myself. We were all fulfilled.

Zig Ziglar said "You can have anything in life you want if you will just help enough other people get what they want." What a concept, helping others achieve success!

NUGGETS FOR THE MIND . . .

"Treat people as if they were what they ought to be and you help them to become what they are capable of being."
 --Goethe

"On your way to the top you will find the journey more pleasant if you help a few friends along---along the way."
 --Sam Spencer

"A sense of purpose and the opportunity to contribute to others -- these are as vital to total health as are adequate nutrition and rest."
 --H. A. Holle, M. D.

"Some citizens are so good that nothing a leader can do will make them better. Others are so incorrigible that nothing can be done to improve them. But the great bulk of the people go with the moral tide of the moment. The leader must help create that tide."
 --Author unknown

"A good boss makes his men realize they have more ability than they think they have so that they consistently do better work than they thought they could."
 --Charles E. Wilson

"When someone sacrifices for another, two people benefit."
 --Philip Spencer

#53 ASK A LOT OF QUESTIONS

One of the most powerful tools you have in life is asking questions of others. This allows you to tap into the knowledge that others have acquired over their years of experience. Questions unlock doors to areas that would not be available to you in any other way.

In my view there are two groups of people who find it difficult to ask questions. First those who are just shy and have trouble speaking to people in general. The other is that category of people who think they know it all or want others to think they know it all and don't want anyone to find out they don't have all the answers. Both are insecure in their different ways. If you fit into one of these two categories of people, find a way out!

Consider your journey through life as your personal university. You are the student, everyone else is the professor. With this perspective and you will find it easier to ask questions. Interesting things happens when you ask questions. You learn something unique. You learn of new places. You experience other view-points, observations, successes, and important facts.

Try this: The next time you meet someone, see how many questions you can ask about them. "Where are you from?" " What is it like there?" "What is one of your most unique experiences?" "What is the most powerful lesson you've learned in life?" Don't be afraid to ask technical questions – "How did you get it to work?" Or "What problems did you encounter?" "How did you overcome them?" None of these questions display ignorance, they show personal interest. Ask these plus other questions then see what you've learned.

NUGGETS FOR THE MIND...

"Judge a man by his questions rather than by his answers."
--Voltaire

"I never learn anything talking. I only learn things from asking questions."
--Lou Holtz

"I attribute the little I know to my not having been ashamed to ask for information, and to my rule of conversation with all descriptions of man of those topics that form their own peculiar professions and pursuits."
--John Locke

"No man really becomes a fool until he stops asking questions."
--Charles Steinmetz

"I am prejudiced in favor of him who, without impudence, can ask boldly. He has faith in humanity, and faith in himself. No one who is not accustomed to giving grandly can ask nobly and with boldness."
--George Santayana

#54 GAIN BALANCE IN YOUR LIFE

Balance keeps things where they should be. Balance is essential for true success.

One day my friend and I were guiding a group of teenage girls along a mountain stream in search of a waterfall. We didn't know exactly where it was, but we knew it was ahead of us. All we had to do was follow the stream. My friend and I would alternate hiking ahead to find the best trail to lead them on. While looking for the best side of the stream along which to guide this large group, we would often cross the stream on a fallen log. Without careful balance someone would invariably fall. They would climb back up on the log, regain their balance and once again carefully cross the stream.

So it is with your life, you must have balance. Balance the physical, emotional, educational, personal, and spiritual areas. Establish balance in your family, employment, and other facets of your life. When you get things out of balance you fall off the log of life. While you are getting back on, you lose both precious time and effort. Everything around you must stop or a least slow down while waiting for you to regain your balance. Once you get back on the log, you must maintain your balance in order to continue. Only when you are back in balance can you walk forward again.

When things are in balance, life runs easier and smoother because we don't have to constantly stop to get things back into balance. It is so important to maintain this stability. The longer you are out of balance, the more difficult it will be to bring yourself back into balance.

NUGGETS FOR THE MIND . . .

"Have a care where there is more sail than ballast."
--William Penn

"Set all things in their proper place, and know that order is the greatest grace."
--William Dryden

"He who has no taste for order, will be often wrong in his judgment, and seldom considerate or conscientious in his actions."
--Lavater

"Life will give you what you ask of her if only you work long enough and hard enough."
--E. Nesbitt

"Common sense is instinct, and enough of it is genius."
--Henry Wheeler Shaw

"Fortunate, indeed, is the man who takes exactly the right measure of himself and holds a just balance between what he can acquire and what he can use."
--Peter Latham

#55 NEVER QUIT · REALIGN – CHANGE FOCUS · CHANGE DEADLINES

I have always said, "You are never a failure until you give up." If you have made an accurate workable plan, your habits will most likely be the reason for not being successful. If your goal is worthwhile, continue to pursue it. Don't quit.

There will be times when your circumstances change some of the elements in your life. You must eliminate the problems, re-align and continue on. If you have given an honest effort, but you didn't meet your deadlines, change the time frame. Keep in mind that the goal is the most important part of the plan.

Imagine that a large super highway is being built, scheduled to be completed in six months. The project is delayed because of a survey problem. Do you cancel the project for that? No! You realign and continue with the project. Next some materials are delivered late. Do you cancel the project because you are delayed? No! You change the deadlines. The project is held up again for political reasons. The six months now have passed, the project is 75% complete. Do you stop and cancel everything because you came short on some internal goals. No! You complete what you started. If it is a worthy goal, finish it!

Many people invest a great deal of time into a project or some form of growth. Then when they come a little short they quit, stop, and abandon it. When you have setbacks, don't quit. Realign, perhaps change your focus, but don't quit!

NUGGETS FOR THE MIND . . .

"If at first you don't succeed, you're running about average. DON'T QUIT."
--Author Unknown

> When things go wrong as they sometimes will,
> And the road you're traveling seems all up-hill;
> When funds are low and debts are high,
> And you want to laugh but you have to sigh;
> When cares are pressing you down a bit,
> Rest if you must -- but don't you quit.

--Author Unknown

"It's when things get rough and you don't quit that success comes."
--Author Unknown

"Success in life depends upon staying power. The reason for failure in most cases is lack of perseverance. Men get tired and give up."
--J.R. Miller

"The difference between perseverance and obstinacy is, that one often comes from a strong will, and the other from a strong won't."
--Henry Ward Beecher

#56 LEARN TO ACCEPT ALL PEOPLE

What a diverse world we live in. We are each uniquely individual. Being different doesn't mean wrong.

A single mother asked me to help in a situation with her two young boys. They were quite upset with each other. They had even exchanged blows and eventually, in the angry exchange one tore up the picture the other was coloring. "What led to all this?" I asked the instigator. "He colored the picture wrong," he responded. "What was wrong?" I continued. "He colored one arm pink," was his answer.

I took the young boy outside to get out of the heated environment. As I continued to settle the boy down I pointed out the other houses in the neighborhood. I said, "Look at the house across the street. Is it wrong because they have flowers and several trees? Or is this one over here wrong because it has no trees or flowers? Maybe yours is wrong because you only have shrubs and bushes. Who is wrong?" Finally he agreed that they were all okay, and, eventually, that it is okay for each of us to be different.

Individualism is the basis of this great nation. People can be different as long as they don't force others to think or believe as they do, nor force others to embrace and participate in their opinions.

Learning to accept all people requires a notable level of tolerance. You should never be required, however, to embrace the unlawful or immoral acts of others as simply "being different." Wrong will always be wrong no mater what costume it adorns!

NUGGETS FOR THE MIND . . .

"So, let us not be blind to differences -- but let us also direct attention to common interests and to the means by which those differences can be resolved. And if we cannot end now differences, at least we can help make the world safe for diversity."
 --John F. Kennedy

"A man should not allow himself to hate even his enemies; because if you indulge this passion on some occasion; it will rise of itself on others. If you hate your enemies; you will contract such a vicious habit of mind as by degrees will break out upon those who are your friends; or those who are indifferent to you."
 --Plutarch

"Getting people to like you is only the other side of liking them."
 --Norman Vincent Peale

"In proportion as our own mind is enlarged we discover a greater number of men of originality. Commonplace people see no difference between one man and another."
 --Pascal

"You can learn a lot from people who view the world differently than you do. "
 --Anthony J. D'Angelo

#57   LOOK FOR SOMETHING GOOD IN EVERYONE

Good can be found in everyone. Sometimes you just have to look a little harder to find it. The objective here, is to find goodness, especially in someone who doesn't agree with you or who perhaps has offended you.

One day I was doing business with a person who was rather difficult to work with. His rude and abrasive style offended me. After he left, I found myself doing what most people do when dealing with someone like that. I began to feel contempt for the man. In a few minutes I was finding fault in everything around me. I had let this negative encounter turn my thoughts negative and it affect me to the point of controlling me.

Several days later I had another occasion to deal with this same abrasive person. This experience began just like our other meetings. After he left, once again, I began to fall into the same trap of negative thinking. But this time I caught myself. I did an abrupt "about face." I tried to look for something good in the man. After a little struggle, I found something. I worked with that thought. The positive thoughts made room for good productive ones. Quickly clearing away the distasteful experience. Soon I was thinking positive thoughts again. The negative cycle was stopped with a positive focus. Equally important, I didn't introduce what could have been a negative attitude to others.

The next time you encounter someone offensive or hard to deal with, try looking for something good. Note the freedom it gives you. You can essentially entertain only one particular thought at a time, so be sure that thought is a good one. Remember: *Thoughts govern attitudes!*

NUGGETS FOR THE MIND . . .

"Nothing is easier than fault-finding; no talent, no self-denial, no brains, no character are required to set up in the grumbling business."
 --Robert West

"The most censorious are generally the least judicious, or deserving, who, having nothing to recommend themselves, will be finding fault with others. -- No man envies the merit of another who has enough of his own."
 --Rule of Life

"There's not the least thing can be said or done, but people will talk and find fault."
 --Miguel de Cervantes

"Maturity is that time when the mirrors in our mind turn to windows and instead of seeing the reflection of ourselves we see others."
 --Author Unknown

"He who has not forgiven an enemy has never yet tasted one of the most sublime enjoyments of life."
 --Lavater

"Confidence in the goodness of another is good proof of one's own goodness."
 --Michel Montaigne

#58 SAY SOMETHING GOOD ABOUT OTHERS

Have you been in a gossip corner lately? Did you enjoy every juicy detail? Did you ever wonder what they said about you when you weren't there? I have seen people's lives ruined by the loose tongue of another. I have seen self esteem drop immediately because of another's thoughtless comments.

I have a friend who finds the very best things to say to everyone with whom he speaks. Perhaps you have a friend like this also. He is always pleasant to be with because of this positive outlook. When I find someone that I enjoy being around, or who makes me feel good, I begin to analyze what it is that makes me feel that way. Then I try to incorporate those uplifting traits into my own life. I have found that if it makes *you* feel good to be treated in a certain way, it certainly will do the same for many others. This idea is one of the qualities I have long labored to implement into my own life.

Try this the next time you are in a gossip corner: say something genuinely good about the person in question, see what happens. You will probably find that others will join in. See if you can single-handedly change the mood to a more uplifting one. When you become proficient at speaking good about others, you will have an abundance of loyal friends. You will also feel extremely good about yourself.

NUGGETS FOR THE MIND . . .

"When a bee stings, she dies. She cannot sting and live. When men sting, their better selves die. Every sting kills a better instinct. Men must not turn bees and kill themselves in stinging others."
--Sir Francis Bacon

"Take my advice, and never draw caricature. -- By the long practice of it I have lost the enjoyment of beauty. -- I never see a face but distorted, and never have the satisfaction to behold the human face divine."
--Hogarth

"The Golden Rule is of no use whatever unless you realize it's your move."
--quoted by Leo Aikman

"Though I speak with the tongues of men and angels and have not charity, I am become as sounding brass, or a tinkling cymbal."
--I Corinthians 13:1-3

"The best time to make friends is before you need them."
--Ethel Barrymore

#59   DON'T PRE-JUDGE

This quality is a very difficult one to develop. The natural human tendency is to judge everything and everyone quickly. Generally, no matter how carefully you judge, you will frequently miss something.

On of my favorite stories is about a trapper who took his wife to Alaska. The wife died leaving him with a two year old son. On some occasions, the father would leave the home for a few hours leaving his son in the care of his trusted dog. On one such trip a terrible storm arose and the father had to take refuge in a hollow tree to save his life. At daybreak he rushed to the cabin. The door was open, his dog was in the corner covered with blood. The father knew just one thing had happened, the hungry dog had turned wolf and killed the child. He saw no alternative; he turned and shot his trusted friend.

He now scanned the bloody scene, furniture torn, the cabin in total disarray. He heard a faint cry from under the bed. It was his son, safe. Now where did all the blood come from? As he searched further, he found the answer in a corner; a dead wolf.

Quick rash judgments can be such a tragedy. Think of this story when you begin to judge others. Ask yourself, "Do I have all the facts?" "Is there more to this than I can see?" "Have I been fair?" Be careful how and when you judge others. Judgment can be so final. You may judge away someone who could be a trusted friend. Remember that others judge you by the same scale that you judge them.

NUGGETS FOR THE MIND . . .

"We judge ourselves by what we feel capable of doing, while others judge us by what we have already done."
  --Henry Wadsworth Longfellow

"Be not angry that you cannot make others as you wish them to be, since you cannot make yourself as you wish to be."
  --Thomas A Kempis

"Looks are so deceptive that people should be done up like food packages with the ingredients clearly labeled."
  --Helen Hudson

"Blessed is the man who has a skin of right thickness. He can work happily in spite of enemies and friends."
  --Henry J. Bailey

"We should behave to our friends as we would wish our friends to behave to us."
  --Aristotle

"Men in general judge more from appearances than from reality. All men have eyes, but few have the gift of penetration."
  --Niccoló Machiavelli

Another Golden Rule: Judge others as you would have others judge you.
  --Sam Spencer

#60   FORMULATE AN HONORABLE REASON WHY THEY ACTED AS THEY DID

One morning I was in a hurrying to be on time for an appointment. I was just about there. Great, I would be on time! One more light and I would be there. As the light turned green, there were three cars ahead of me to make a left turn. I found myself coaching the drivers so I could make it on this light. I said, "Go! Go now!" "Why didn't you go?" Two cars finally went, The one in front of me waited at the crosswalk. I said, "Scoot up, let me squeeze in behind you." She couldn't hear me. The light turned yellow, "Get out there!" I yelled in frustration. The light turned red, we were both still at the light. I could see she was an elderly lady. I began to use this idea. "I'll bet she is scared to death of this traffic coming 50 miles an hour towards her. She probably has a difficult time judging distance. She's probably a widow with nobody to help her with life's problems."

As these "honorable" reasons raced through my mind I had just about convinced myself to jump out and lend a hand when the light turned green. We both safely made it through the light. I was on time and with a good attitude. I will never know the real story of this woman's life, and it doesn't matter, but just having generous thoughts about her made my own day better.

This idea helps me immensely, especially when I get into a situation where someone has done something to me that disturbed me in some way. I try to formulate an honorable reason why they would do as they did. I create empathy in my mind for them and then avoid the unhealthy negative emotions that would otherwise have gone through my mind.

NUGGETS FOR THE MIND . . .

"There is so much good in the worst of us, and so much bad in the best of us, it's hard to tell which one of us ought to reform the rest of us."
 --Author Unknown

"There never was a bad man that had ability for good service."
 --Edmund Burke

"Beware, so long as you live, of judging men by their outward appearance."
 --La Fontaine

"Never does a man portray his own character more vividly than in his manner of portraying another."
 --Jean Paul Richter

"Men are created that they may live for each other, teach them to be better or bear them as they are."
 --Marcus Aurelius

"Make it a practice to judge persons and things in the most favorable light at all times and under all circumstances."
 --St. Vincent de Paul

#61 SAY "HELLO" TO STRANGERS

Speaking of winning friends, Dale Carnegie said, "Why not study the technique of the greatest winner of friends the world has ever known?" He then begins to talk about dogs. I love dogs, don't you? They make you feel like you're the only person in the world. When they see you they wag their tails and jump up an down with excitement. They can't wait to be a part of your life. Be more like the friendly dogs and show a genuine interest in everyone you see.

Mr. Carnegie also said, "You can make more friends in two months by becoming interested in other people than you can in two years of trying to get other people interested in you."

Try just a simple "Hello, how are you?" or "Pretty day, isn't it?" Any kind of recognition to another brightens up their day. Do it with a smile, with sincere intent to make *their* day brighter. Before long you will have a reputation of being a friendly person, and people will want to become your friend.

This is such a simple little thing, but what an impact it will make in your life and the lives of those you meet. Try it for a few days. First practice a few salutations. Then when you hit the streets, office buildings, elevators or wherever you meet people, begin to say hello! In a few weeks you'll notice a difference in your life. It will be a really positive one!

If you have trouble with this one, you might start with the people you know and then graduate to strangers.

NUGGETS FOR THE MIND . . .

"It takes a wise man to recognize a wise man."
 --Xenophanes

"Divine Love always has met and always will meet every human need."
 --Mary Baker Eddy

"A stale article, if you dip it in a good, warm, sunny smile, will go off better than a fresh one that you've scowled upon."
 --Nathaniel Hawthorne

"Be kind--remember every one you meet is fighting a battle--everybody's lonesome."
 --Marrion Parker

"Have you had a kindness shown? Pass it on."
 --Henry Burton

"Start some kind word on it's travels. There is no telling where the good you may do will stop."
 --Sir Wilfred Grenfell

"A 'hello' a day keeps the shrink away!"
 --Sam Spencer

#62   BE COURTEOUS TO OTHERS

Courtesy is more than being kind to others, it is also showing respect and consideration. If you are a courteous person you will allow others to finish talking before you speak, you will be polite when others are rude. Courtesy goes beyond general kindness. It includes respect for being a human being.

Your mother probably said, "If you can't say something nice, then don't say anything at all." Speaking nicely is one way of being courteous. You don't have to choose only the elderly lady to open the door, nor the beauty queen. You can open the door for men and children, or even someone you may not particularly like. The other day I opened the door for a patrolman as we entered the same place of business. You can let another person slip in on the freeway. There are many ways to be courteous. How many can you identify?

Consider these ways to be courteous, and add dozens more:

   ...Wait for your turn.
   ...Open the door for others.
   ...Hold the elevator door open.
   ...Let others off first.
   ...Allow another driver to enter the traffic.
   ...If you smoke, watch your smoke.
   ...Keep your grocery cart to the side of the aisle

As you begin to implement courtesy you will establish a general attitude of thinking of others and showing them respect. Develop a habit of asking yourself, "Am I being courteous, how can I be courteous?"

NUGGETS FOR THE MIND . . .

"Happiness is a hard thing because it is achieved only by making others happy."
 --Stuart Cloete

"The highest exercise of charity is charity towards the uncharitable."
 --J. S. Buckminster

"You don't have to blow out the other fellow's light to let your own shine."
 --Bernard Baruch

"No man is a true gentleman who does not inspire the affection and devotion of his servants."
 --Andrew Carnegie

"Be pleasant until ten o'clock in the morning and the rest of the day will take care of itself."
 --Elbert Hubbard

"You have not fulfilled every duty unless you have fulfilled that of being cheerful and pleasant."
 --C.C. Buxton

#63 REWARD YOURSELF

Have you ever won a prize, or been recognized for special effort? How did you feel? I'm certain you felt fulfilled, with a desire to do even better. Rewards are a way of motivating and showing appreciation. Incentive programs are earned rewards that motivate a person to greater achievement. To keep yourself motivated, practice giving yourself incentives and rewards for a job well done. Give yourself something to look forward to.

There was an occasion in my life when I was about as low as I'd ever been. No motivation, no desire to do anything about it. A friend told me that he felt I needed to rebuild my self-esteem with some small successes and give myself a reward for good results. He was right. I set a very simple goal. I told myself that upon completion I would get a particular reward. My task took much longer than it normally would have, but I kept working until I was finished. Having reached the goal, I earned the reward and my self-esteem increased.

This worked. I began to do more of these little "achieve and reward" exercises. Before long I had come to the point where I was feeling much better about myself. I was able to rebuild my self-esteem a little at a time.

Give yourself rewards for your own good efforts. Tell yourself you can't go to the movie (reward) or play golf (reward) until you have finished the dishes (task) or set five appointments (task). You don't need a reward for everything you do, but you do need them often enough to sustain motivation and maintain the joy of achieving. Tasks must be reasonable and achievable, based on your ability. Rewards must be something you will enjoy.

NUGGETS FOR THE MIND . . .

"Wisdom is the reward you get for a lifetime of listening when you'd preferred to talk."
 --Doug Larson

"Antiquity is enjoyed not by the ancients who lived in the infancy of things, but by us who live in their maturity."
 --Colton

"The reward for being true to a correct principle is worth whatever it costs, and often the greatest reward is the character development in the person who remains true."
 --Author Unknown

"The highest reward for a man's toil is not what he gets from it, but what he becomes by it."
 --Author Unknown

"Success or failure depends more upon attitude than upon capacity...successful men act as though they have accomplished or are enjoying something. Soon it becomes a reality. Act, look, feel successful, conduct yourself accordingly, and you will be amazed at the positive results."
 --Dr. DuPree Jordan, Jr.

#64 TAKE TIME FOR YOURSELF

Time for yourself should be taken as often as you feel needful. The tendency is to get this area of your life out of balance first, too much or too little. If you are constantly around others you will never really get to know who you are. However a word of caution; don't use this as an excuse to run away from your problems or responsibilities.

Take an opportunity to shop by yourself, to read what you want to read, to go where you want to go or to visit whom you want to visit. You can get so caught up in helping others or in being told what to do, you forget to take time to tend to your own needs. Another pitfall is becoming so involved in your work or other projects that you neglect the very person who gets the work done, yourself. This may be the reminder you have been needing. Remember, if you don't take time for yourself, the time you give to others will soon become a burden.

When you take time for yourself you will get a genuine perspective on life. You will see more clearly with your own eyes. You will feel self-fulfilled. You will find new energy. When I take time for myself, I get a clearer perspective. I find a new determination to face my challenges and a greater ability to do my work with a good attitude.

I look at it this way: When I injure my body I give it a rest and allow it time to heal. To keep me emotionally healthy, sometimes I just need some time for myself away from troubles.

NUGGETS FOR THE MIND . . .

"It is doing some service to humanity, to amuse innocently. They know but little of society who think we can bear to be always employed, either in duties or meditation, without relaxation."
--H. More

"Find out for yourself the form of rest that refreshes you best."
--Daniel Considine

"Try as much as to be wholly alive, with all your might, and when you laugh, laugh like hell and when you get angry, get good and angry. Try to be alive. You will be dead soon enough."
--William Saroyan

"Live all you can; it's a mistake not to. It doesn't so much matter what you do in particular so long as you have your life."
--Henry James

"Sometimes the most urgent and vital thing you can possibly do is take a complete rest."
--Author Unknown

"I'll be okay in a little while, but for now, just give me some space."
--Ruth Cardinali

#65 RECOGNIZE THAT PROBLEMS ARE A PART OF LIFE - USE THEM TO GROW

The key word here is *recognize*. Some people are stymied by problems and get frustrated or upset when a problem interferes with life. No matter how you look at the problem, no matter how upset you get, the problem doesn't go away until something is done to remedy it.

I enjoy playing with ants. They are fascinating insects; ants don't let anything stop their progress. I put my foot down in the path and they just go around with no hesitation. If they can't go around, they will go over; if not over then under. Ants never lose a step no matter what obstacle they face. If their heavy load is knocked off they merely stop, pick it up and continue on their way. I have never seen an ant stomp his feet, jump up and down or yell and curse the problem it faced. Nor have I ever seen an ant stop, turn around and go home crying! What a great attribute, always moving forward!

As problems arise try some self talk by using the following phrases:

...That's just part of life.
...I can't change it so I'll just get working on it.
...This is just one of those things that happens to others. -- I guess now, I'm just "one of the others."

Master this idea and with each problem, think of it as a part of life's process and your attitude will change. Be more like the ants, and you won't miss a step either.

NUGGETS FOR THE MIND . . .

"You can bear anything if it isn't your own fault."
--Katherine Fullerton Gerould

"The quality of a man's life is dependent upon his strength of will to accept or reject the issues of life, not as he wants them to be, but as they are."
--Paul A. Anderson

"It's not the problem that builds character in a man, but how he handles the problem."
--Sam Spencer

"Difficulties elicit talents that in more fortunate circumstances would lie dormant."
--Horace

"Use your gift faithfully and they shall be enlarged. Practice what you know, and you shall attain higher knowledge."
--Sir Edwin Arnold

"To most men, experience is like the stern lights of a ship which illumine only the track it has passed."
--Samuel Taylor Coleridge

"Don't just stand there! Do something - even if it's right."
--Gene Spencer

#66 SLEEP ON IT AND LET THE SUBCONSCIOUS CREATE

The subconscious is a quiet workhorse, always working on solutions for the problems you give it. Have you ever experienced a flash in your conscious that revealed a solution to a problem you had been pondering? This is the subconscious answering your needs.

I rely on my subconscious to enlarge my thinking capacity. There are several things I do to stimulate my subconscious creativity.

Let me suggest you try these few activities:

...During the day meditate and ponder the problem, entertain all solutions; good, bad, even ridiculous.
...Don't develop them yet, keep your thoughts light.
...Take time to write solutions to major problems.
...Don't take pot shots at your ideas yet.
...Before you go to bed, run the ideas through your mind, don't worry about them, just think about them.
...Verbally tell yourself that you are going to let your subconscious mind take over the problem and then mentally leave it alone.

I find that this process has helped me to wake up with fresh ideas, solutions, and areas to consider. Be ready to write them down because you can lose them fast. The subconscious will do so much for you if you only allow it to do so. Give your subconscious a chance. It's all yours.

NUGGETS FOR THE MIND...

"When I have nothing to do for an hour, and I don't want to do anything, I neither read nor watch television, I sit back in a chair and let my mind relax. I do what I call Idling. It's as if the motorcar's running but you haven't got it in gear. You have to allow a certain amount of time in which you are doing nothing in order to have things occur to you, to let your mind think."
  --Mortimer Adler

"One of the greatest pains to human nature is the pain of a new idea."
  --George F. Baer

"Neither man or nation can exist without a sublime idea."
  --Feodor Dostoevski

"A man dies daily, only to be reborn in the morning, bigger, better and wiser."
  --Emmett Fox

"Use your gifts faithfully and they shall be enlarged. Practice what you know, and you shall attain higher knowledge."
  --Sir Edwin Arnold

#67 RECOGNIZE THE CONTRIBUTIONS OF OTHERS IN YOUR LIFE

Whatever you have achieved, someone else most certainly helped you gain it. These people are a necessary part of your success. They were with you when you needed a hand. They pop in and out from time to time and give you a little boost. Remember who assisted you in arriving where you are today. Give them the credit they deserve both privately and publicly.

Coach Paul "Bear" Bryant, the great football coach said; "I'm just a plow hand from Arkansas, But I have learned how to hold a team together. How to lift some men up, how to calm down others, until finally they've got one heartbeat together, a team. There's just three things I'd ever say:
    If anything goes bad, I did it.
    If anything goes semi-good, then we did it.
    If anything goes real good, then you did it.
That's all it takes to get people to win football games for you."

When credit is given to another for a job well done, two hearts are warmed: the one who received the credit as well as the one who gave the credit. I have found that when I include others in my success, success is always sweeter.

Be fair in giving credit to others. Often it is difficult to praise those whom you may not like. Now your courage and integrity come into action. This is a quality of great, yet humble, people. This virtue can be yours with just a little effort.

NUGGETS FOR THE MIND

"If you have no friends to share or rejoice in your success in life -- if you can not look back to those to whom you owe gratitude, or forward to those to whom you ought to afford protection, still it is no less incumbent on you to move steadily in the path of duty: for your active exertions are due not only to society; but in humble gratitude to the Being who made you a member of it, with powers to serve yourself and others."
 --Walter Scott

"An old colored brother is said to have finished his prayer with words like these: 'And now good Lord; I know that you ain't goen to let nothing come to me that me and you together can't handle."
 --Author Unknown

"All great things are only a number of small things that have carefully been collected together."
 --Author Unknown

"For the strength of the Pack is the Wolf, and the strength of the Wolf is the Pack."
 --Author unknown

"Your life is made up of little bits and pieces from other people."
 --Sam Spencer

#68   TAKE TIME TO SMELL THE ROSES

One day I was walking home from church with my girls. As we passed a friend's house they saw the beautiful rose bushes with roses in full bloom. My friend, Brian, cut them each a rose. The rest of the way home they couldn't stop smelling the roses. The roses in your life are the things which give pleasure and satisfaction. That which gives comfort and cheer; the good times you want to always remember. The things which make the tough times pass more easily. Things that fulfill you

Yes, the roses are out there. Sometimes you have to look to find them. Take time to reflect on all the good things that are a part of your life. On occasion, late at night when everyone is in bed, I have found myself walking through my house looking at all the wonderful things in my life. Then I find myself looking in on my family as they sleep and thinking of the joy they bring into my life and home. I then reflect on the support and many good qualities they bring to the entire family. I think of my work and what it provides me and my family. Whenever I take time to smell the roses, I grow closer to others and appreciate what I have. In my heart I thank God and feel a warm, inner peace.

You, too, have done this in the past and felt that enriched feeling. It must be done often enough to increase your appreciation and stimulate a zest for life. This is a habit you need to develop and then continually ask yourself, "Do I need to take time to smell the roses?" Just take the time, often that is the only way you will get it. Schedule time for yourself to go to your quiet place and smell the roses.

NUGGETS FOR THE MIND...

"Self denial is not negative repression but the cost of positive achievement."
 --Harry Emerson Fosdick

"In the name of God, stop a moment, cease your work, look around you...."
 --Leo Tolstoy

"Take a rest; a field that has rested gives a bountiful crop."
 --Ovid

"Get pleasure out of life....as much as you can. Nobody ever died from pleasure."
 --Sol Hurok

"The foolish man seeks happiness in the distant, the wise grows it under his feet."
 --James Oppenheim

"Take time to smell the roses, they are short lived. Soon they will dry up, crumble and fade into the past, quietly becoming a distant memory."
 --Sam Spencer

#69 TRY TO HAVE FUN

You can either enjoy what you have to do, you can hate it or something in between. You will decide which.

One day one of my daughters came to me and said, "Daddy, play Barbies with me, it'll be fun." Although I was busy, I sensed she needed some of my time. I consented. She began to lay out the rules, "Dad you be Ken because you're the man. Here, you can dress him. Do you want to go on a picnic or to the movies? You drive." The instructions kept coming. Many times I had watched the girls go through this sacred ritual. I knew my part well and performed it to perfection but with the reluctance of most males, (I was Ken).

She then said, "Come on dad, just try to have fun!" My mind had been on the many other things I felt I should be doing. She recognized that I wasn't having fun. Then I decided that I needed to change my attitude and try to have fun. Within minutes, I was having fun! What did I learn? Something I already knew. If you are going to be doing something anyway, why not have fun doing it. It's all in your attitude.

As you run into daily tasks that you just don't enjoy, find something you like about your task. Nobody is telling you, except yourself, to dislike what you are doing. Find some kind of game or strategy to help you like what you are doing or just think how good you will feel when you are completed. Sing a song or listen to music you like. When you are having fun your day will go faster and you will have a better attitude. So -- "Just try to have fun!"

NUGGETS FOR THE MIND . . .

"The happiness of every country depends upon the character of its people, rather than the form of its government."
 --Thomas Chandler Haliburton

"I never did a days' work in my life -- it was all fun."
 --Thomas A. Edison

"Nothing is more fun than to have a little more to do than you get through with.
 --William Wrighley

"Our Creator would never have made such lovely days, and have given us the deep hearts to enjoy them, above and beyond all thought, unless we were meant to be immortal."
 --Nathaniel Hawthorne

"Seek not, my soul, the life of the immortals; but enjoy to the full the resources that are within thy reach."
 --Pindar

"How little we should enjoy life if we never flattered ourselves."
 --Duc de La Rochefoucauld

#70 ASK YOURSELF, "WHAT AM I SUPPOSE TO BE DOING HERE AND NOW?"

What you do with your time is a challenge that you must face every day. What to do next can be your constant concern. "What am I *supposed* to be doing here and now?" The answer to this question will help greatly in your time management. If you know where you are supposed to be, then be there. If you know what you should be doing, then do it.

I had a few insurance agents who often took a long time getting ready to go out to sell, and took a long time getting back. Little distractions and excuses to waste time frequently destroyed their productivity. They knew what they should have been doing, they knew where they were supposed to be, but they lacked the self-discipline to follow through. You cannot expect success to occur when you are not where you should be, doing what you should be doing.

You may not be the most talented person; you may not be a walking encyclopedia. But if you are where you are suppose to be and doing what you are suppose to be doing, you will not only avoid future trouble, but ultimately you will meet success.

Remember, when it is time, success will be where it is suppose to be. Consider this thought, "Do what you ought, not what you please." (Author Unknown)

NUGGETS FOR THE MIND . . .

"It is a good and safe rule to sojourn in every place as if you meant to spend your life there; never omitting an opportunity of doing a kindness; or speaking a true word; or making a friend."
 --John Ruskin

"The quality of a man's life is in direct proportion to his commitment to excellence regardless of his chosen field of endeavor."
 --Vince Lombardi

"Every individual has a place to fill in the world, and is important in some respect, whether he chooses to be so or not."
 --Nathaniel Hawthorne

"Have a time and a place for everything, and do everything in its time and place, and you will not only accomplish more, but have far more leisure than those who are always hurrying, as if vainly attempting to overtake time that had been lost."
 --Tyron Edwards

"It is best to do things systematically, since we are only human, and disorder is our worst enemy."
 --Hesiod

#71 ACCENTUATE THE POSITIVE - LEARN FROM THE NEGATIVE

Every cloud has a silver lining. Sometimes you need to really stretch to find it, but if you continually find the positive in situations, your life will be happier and more serene.

A gentleman passing by a little league game stopped to ask the score of one of the young players.

"We're behind 18 to nothing," the boy responded.

"We'll you don't look discouraged," returned the gentleman.

"Why should I be discouraged, we have last bats."

Take a lesson from the young boy and look at the positive side. At times you can be so caught up in the negative you can't see any positive. If, as you look out the window into your life, every day seems overcast and dreary, consider cleaning your window. Eliminate the negative. Give yourself a brighter perspective by looking at and for the positive.

I heard a story of a duck hunter who found the perfect dog. This dog could "walk on water." One day the hunter took a friend hunting. He sent the dog, walking on the water, to retrieve duck after duck. At the end of the day the hunter asked his friend if he had noticed anything different about his dog. His friend answered, "Yes, I noticed he couldn't swim."

Accentuate the positive! Keep your "windows to the world" clean to maintain a brighter perspective on life.

NUGGETS FOR THE MIND . . .

"Don't worry if your job is small and your rewards few. Remember that the mighty oak was once a nut like you." -
-Author Unknown

"There are two modes of acquiring knowledge, namely by reasoning and experience. Reasoning draws a conclusion and makes us grant the conclusion, but does not make the conclusion certain, nor does it remove doubt so that the mind may rest on the intuition of truth, unless the mind discovers it by the path of experience."
--Roger Bacon

"We should never despair if our situation before has been unpromising and has changed for the better, so I trust, it will again. If new difficulties arise, we must only put forth new exertions and proportion our efforts to the exigency of the times."
--General George Washington

"Good habits are as easy to form as bad ones."
--Tim McCarver

"Do not let what you cannot do interfere with what you can do."
--Author Unknown

#72 ACT AND DRESS AS THE SITUATION REQUIRES

When most people meet you for the first time, their impression is generally based on your outward appearance and your demeanor. They don't know the inside yet. To truly get to know someone will take some time.

When you walk into someone's house or office to do business, if your clothing is not as neat as it should be, or it doesn't match your message, what kind of an impression are you giving them? You should be careful not to over dress or under dress. Know what the occasion requires. Put yourself in the other person's position. Ask yourself, "Would I hire this person?" "Would I do business with this person?" "Is this person one I would want to be seen with?" First make these judgments, then make necessary adjustments.

To illustrate how appearance can influences others, think about this story; I was shopping for a lap top computer, and visited a computer store near my plant. Having worked all day, I was dressed in dusty Levis and a tee shirt. I did not appear to be the type of person who was successful enough to buy anything so pricey. The few times I was in that store I never even received any sales attention. A friend who was dressed in office attire went into the same store and was treated quite the opposite. What do you think was the difference?

Consider this. You see two salespeople in front of your house. Both have a similar product, but one is very well dressed and well mannered, the other is a little sloppy. With whom would you choose to do business? Whom would you hire? Get the vision! Be that person!

NUGGETS FOR THE MIND . . .

"We act the way we dress. Neglected and untidy clothes reflect a neglected and untidy mind."
--Author Unknown

"What we do upon some great occasion will probably depend on what we already are; and what we will be the result of self-discipline."
--H. P. Liddon

"Keeping your clothes well pressed will keep you from looking hard pressed."
--Coleman Cox

"Your first appearance, he said to me, is the gauge by which you will be measured; try to manage that you may go beyond yourself in after times, but beware of ever doing less."
--Jean Jacques Rousseau

"There's more to it than looking your best. You have to be at your best, too -- boring along all the time, happy, upbeat, friendly."
--Farrah Fawcett

"Of all the things you wear, your expression is the most important."
--John Ruskin

#73 DON'T SPEND IT UNTIL YOU HAVE EARNED IT

This idea doesn't need much explanation; it requires discipline, action and commitment. This particularly applies to the frills and extras. When you start the trend of living outside of your means, you tread a very dangerous path. What would you do if you lost your job, or had some emergency? If you are obliged to pay for something you really didn't need you could have trouble. Good financial planning is essential for a happy, successful life.

Get a handle on your income and expenses. Don't let other people, fads, trends or personal desires trap you outside of your income. Save a little for a rainy day. Keep yourself prepared financially for emergencies. Have a cushion between your income and expenses.

One of my daughters, at 15, learned to stretch her money by buying clothes on sale, putting them on lay-a-way, and paying as she earned the money. Become creative in satisfying your needs. Consider used items when purchasing cars, stereos or other extras. This can be an option that will save you money and also satisfy your present needs. Trading is another excellent way to conserve capital. Consider trading with someone for goods and services you both need.

Take charge of your finances, analyze your needs, study your wants. Learn to say "NO" to extras.

NUGGETS FOR THE MIND . . .

"There is nothing so habit-forming as money."
 --Don Marquis

"If you know how to spend less than you get, you have the philosopher's stone."
 --Benjamin Franklin

"If you would be wealthy, think of saving as well as of getting; the Indies have not made Spain rich, because her outgoes are greater than her incomes."
 --Benjamin Franklin

"For age and want, save while you may;
No morning sun lasts a whole day."
 --Benjamin Franklin

"All progress is based upon the universal innate desire on the part of every organism to live beyond its income."
 --Samuel Butler

"If you want to get rich, save what you get. A fool can earn money, but it takes a wise man to save and dispose of it to his own advantage."
 --Brigham Young

#74 PREPARE AND PLAN FOR PITFALLS

In your planning and problem solving, you must also consider the pitfalls. This is not thinking about the negative, it is safeguarding against misfortune.

When you go on a fifty mile bike ride, you make the necessary preparations, taking food, water, plan the route, etc. However, you also plan for pitfalls. You carry tools and patches in the event of a flat tire or break down. You may carry a poncho in case of rain. Another item you certainly take is a first aid kit. You may never need the extra items you have taken, however, planning for pitfalls is just a good practice and will give you a greater peace of mind.

Use the same principal as you travel through life's challenges, as you set goals and make plans. Look ahead to identify the pitfalls. Plan what you will do in such an event. As you familiarize yourself with potential pitfalls you will recognize what you can do to avoid the problem. In the event an unexpected problem arises, you will be mentally practiced to face it.

Keeping yourself well informed is another way to prepare for future pitfalls. As you read and study what others have done with their lives situations, you can increase your problem solving knowledge to draw on in the future.

Avoid frustration; think ahead · look ahead · plan ahead!

NUGGETS FOR THE MIND . . .

"It takes less time to do a thing right than to explain why you did it wrong."
 --Author Unknown

"Prudence will carry a man all over the world, but the impetuous will find every step difficult."
 --Lao Tse

"We are made strong by the difficulties we face not by those we evade."
 --Author Unknown

"The greater the difficulty the more glory in surmounting it. Skillful pilots gain their reputation from storms and tempests."
 --Epicurus

"Adversity is a severe instructor, set over us by one who knows us better than we do ourselves, as he loves us better too. He that wrestles with us strengthens our nerves and sharpens our skill. Our antagonist is our helper. This conflict with difficulty makes us acquainted with our object, and compels us to consider it in all its relations. It will not suffer us to be superficial."
 --Burke

#75 TAKE A FEW MINUTES TO ASK; "WHAT HAVE I LEARNED FROM THIS SITUATION?"

At times I have done something that proved later to be a poor a decision. Occasionally I have found myself greatly chagrined by a misjudgment that I had made. Other times I have cost myself time and money. This can happen to anyone - family members, co-workers or friends.

Once you have corrected the problem, it is time to do some preventative maintenance, to learn. Here are some steps to consider for yourself and maybe for others involved:

...Identify the events that lead to this result.
...Don't place blame, just analyze.
...What could have been done to prevent the situation?
...Be sure you emphasize *next time*. You cannot change the past. Accept it, obtain knowledge and information from it, then let it go.
...Discuss what you can do to avert a recurrence.

Most importantly, after underestimating the outcome, ask questions that cast no blame. Remember, you need to learn without injuring yourself or others. Recognize that you cannot correct the past by harsh words or actions.

An understanding, nonjudgmental attitude will result in respect and the best situation. To learn from all situations is more important than all other factors.

NUGGETS FOR THE MIND . . .

Yes, experience is a great teacher,
If we learned all the good from experience
And the bad from just "being told."
 --Dean Nethercott Olson

"Experience keeps a dear school, but fools will learn in no other, and scarce in that."
 --Benjamin Franklin

"A man learns to skate by staggering about making a fool of himself; Indeed he progresses in all things by making a fool of himself."
 --George Bernard Shaw

"Acquire Knowledge whilst thinking over the old, and you may become a teacher of others."
 --Confucius

"We should live and learn; but by the time we've learned, it's too late to live."
 --Carolyn Wells

"Each billow that comes rolling on to toss us on its crest,
Is nature's way to teach us how to do our level best.
If we learn each trial's lesson, 'tis an aid our lives to guide,
If we pass it by unheeded, we're just drifting with the tide.
So when trials and tribulations come to fill your mind with doubt,
They're to teach some needed lesson you could never learn without."
 --Author Unknown

#76 SING AND LISTEN TO "FEEL GOOD" SONGS

If you want to be happy, then do happy things. This is an idea that can lift your spirits whenever you need a little lift. Music is the universal language of feelings. You can control and change your emotions by the strategic use of music. How often have you come home after a hard day and just turned on the stereo, laid back and soothed the soul?

Music is meant to move and inspire. Consider this question, "What does your music inspire you to do?" Music can keep you company; music can relax you; music can help time move more quickly. You have a limited amount of time in each day, so when you take time for music, be sure it does positive things for you and your attitude.

Ask yourself, "Does the music I listen to motivate me?" "Does it make me feel good?" Also, "Does the music I listen to, inspire me like I would like it to?" The music you listen to throughout your day will determine your attitude and your attitude determines success. There are many different types of music. Try different varieties. You may find that there are other types of music you like. Analyze how each one makes you feel and use music to help you "feel good!" Choose the music you listen to, to augment your performance.

NUGGETS FOR THE MIND . . .

"Music is well said to be the speech of angels."
 --Thomas Carlyle

"She poured out the liquid music of her voice to quench the thirst of her spirit."
 --Nathaniel Hawthorne

"A bell is no bell "til you ring it. A song is no song "til you sing it. And love in your heart wasn't put there to stay, Love isn't love 'til you give it away."
 --Oscar Hammerstein

"One ought, every day at least, to hear a little song, read a good poem, see a fine picture, and, if it were , to speak a few reasonable words."
 --Johann W. von Goethe

> "How many of us ever stop to think
> Of music as a wondrous magic link
> With God; taking sometimes the place of prayer,
> When words have failed us 'neath the weight of care'
> Music, that knows no country, race or creed;
> But gives to each according to his need."
> --Author Unknown

#77   DON'"T QUARREL WITH OTHERS

No one ever wins in a quarrel. In fact both lose. My father would always say, "Boys who fight, both lose." How do you both lose? One may get the best of the other physically. One may go home with torn clothes or a bloody nose. But most likely they will both go home losers, possibly with hurt feelings that may never heal.

Think of the times you've argued. Did you leave feeling good? How often did you feel like the loser?

Before you get into an argument, ask yourself:

...It is really worth quarreling over?
...What will I really gain?
...If I win, what will I also lose?
...How will this effect my day?
...Is the harm I will cause worth it?
...Am I willing to accept the short and long term consequences?

Once you have examined the real results of quarreling, you will see there are better ways. Being aware of the view point of others, you will help in finding ways to work things out. Take the lead on this one, if you don't get into the quarrel, there won't be one. If the other person persist, just walk away, it takes two to quarrel.

Never be afraid to walk away, you can always return at a better time. Take the good advise from the Bible -- Just "turn the other cheek" and walk away.

NUGGETS FOR THE MIND...

"I never take my own side in a quarrel."
--Robert Frost

'He that blows the coals in quarrels he has nothing to do with has no right to complain if the sparks fly in his face."
--Benjamin Franklin

"Two cannot fall out if one does not choose."
--Spanish Proverb

"People generally quarrel because they cannot argue."
--Gilbert K. Chesterton

"When we quarrel, how we wish we had been blameless!"
--Ralph Waldo Emerson

"Those who in quarrels interpose,
 Must often wipe a bloody nose."
--John Gay

"I have noticed that when chickens quit quarreling over their food, they often find that there is enough for all of them. I wonder if it might not be the same with the human race."
--Don Marquis

#78 HAVE A PLAN FOR EACH DAY, WEEK, MONTH, YEAR

Planning is the key to success. Success doesn't happen by chance. If you want to find success, you must think ahead, set goals for the year, then break them down to goals for the month, the week and finally for each day. This tiered planning will give you direction. Direction will lead to action. Action will lead to success. It is difficult to go any farther than your plan, so be sure your plan is laid out far enough to take you where your aspirations are.

Each day before you get started, write down the things you need to do for that day. Organize the list and there is your plan. Having a plan is just that simple. Now take time to write down what you would like to do this week. With this list, formulate the steps to achieve your goal. Do the same thing for the month. Now follow the steps for the year.

Most people say they have plans, but never take time to write them down. Writing your plans down will do at least two things for you:

...Store a message for the subconscious to work on
...Increase your personal commitment to perform.

I remember as a teenager a teacher often saying, "If you fail to plan, then plan to fail."

Take time to plan. You will accomplish more.

NUGGETS FOR THE MIND . . .

"The years teach much which the days never know."
--Ralph Waldo Emerson

"Most people are in favor of progress, it's the changes they don't like."
--Author Unknown

"When desire and will and work move together, in the right direction, nothing can stop us."
--Author Unknown

"There is no point at which having arrived we can remain."
--Author Unknown

"Today's progress was yesterday's plan."
--Author Unknown

"If you don't know where you are going, you will never know when you've arrived."
--Sam Spencer

"Patton's Law: A good plan today is better than a perfect plan tomorrow."
--Author Unknown

#79   DO HARD THINGS FIRST

When you have a choice, often times it is best to do the hard things first. This is a technique I learned very early in my life. When eating dinner I would first eat my vegetables and then progress through the meal to my meat, eating what I felt to be, the best things last. As I progressed to the end, my food got better and better.

I do exactly the same in my daily tasks. Whenever I do the more difficult and unpleasant tasks first. You always have your best energy at the beginning of whatever you do, and need to attack the toughest things when your energy is high. Once the hard work is out of the way, all other tasks become easier. You will find that when you do the unpleasant tasks first, you will be anxiously working to get to the more pleasant ones. This will lead to a better attitude, and a better attitude will lead to greater efficiency. When you finish, you will find that you will still have good energy.

Conversely, if you do the easiest and most pleasant tasks first you will dread the tasks to come. You will likely drag through the pleasant task and probably not even enjoy them, dreading what is to come. So to make it very simple:

...Make a list of what you have to do.
...Order them from most distasteful or difficult to the easiest
...Begin with the toughest tasks and work towards the simpler chores.

This really works!

NUGGETS FOR THE MIND . . .

"Settle one difficulty, and you keep a hundred others away."
  --Confucius

"Victories that are cheap are cheap. Those only are worth having which come as the result of hard fighting."
  --Henry Ward Beecher

"A hard beginning maketh a good ending."
  --John Heywood

"The art of winning in business is in working hard -- not taking things too seriously."
  --Elbert Hubbard

"The man of virtue makes the difficulty to be overcome his first business, and success only a subsequent consideration."
  --Confucius

"What do we live life for if not to make life less difficult for others?"
  --George Eliot

#80   GIVE FIVE MINUTES MORE

Such a simple thing - give five minutes more. This is like going the proverbial "extra mile." Give five minutes more at work, in service organizations, or helping a neighbor. You not only feel great about yourself, but others gain a greater respect for you. Some people might mock one who always gives a little extra, but don't let this discourage you. Rise above the ridicule. Remember that you are in control of your life not anyone else.

With five minutes more you will feel fulfilled because you have given more than a fair and honest effort. Let it never be said of you that you short changed anyone.

Larry Bird, one of the greatest basketball players of all time would always come to practice early and would usually stay a little late. That little extra was one of the habits he developed that made him great.

Try this for the next thirty days without letting anyone know what you're doing. Do it at work, do it at church, do it in your dealings with everyone; lend a helping hand just five minutes more than expected. You will find a new attitude in your life, you will get more respect from your associates, and, more importantly, your self- esteem will increase.

NUGGETS FOR THE MIND . . .

"Sufficient to today are the duties of today. Don't waste life in doubts and fears; spend yourself on the work before you; well assured that the right performance of this hour's duties will be the best preparation for the hours or ages that follow it."
 --Ralph Waldo Emerson

"We are not sent into the world to do anything into which we cannot put our hearts. We have certain work to do for our own bread, and that is to be done strenuously; other work to do for our delight, and that is to be done heartily. Neither is to be done by halves, but with a will, and what is not worth this effort is not to be done at all."
 --John Ruskin

"When a lady once asked Turner, the celebrated English painter, what his secret was, he replied, 'I have no secret, madam, but hard work. This is the secret that many never learn, and they do not succeed because they do not learn it. Labor is the genius which changes the world from ugliness to beauty and the great curse to a blessing."
 --Author Unknown

#81 LEARN TO SAY GOOD-BYE

Saying good-bye can be a very hard thing to do. People want to hold on to the security of the past and still be able to live in the future. This kind of person will struggle to find real happiness. The past is gone; you are living today. In order to go to a new city, you must leave the one you are in. In order to reach tomorrow you must leave yesterday.

When you let go, you make room for progress. You are no longer letting memories of the past control tomorrow. I am not saying to forget the past, some nostalgic event, a friend, or a family member. Keep pleasant memories, but that was yesterday, it cannot be relived. This is today!

Think of it as climbing stairs. Each step you take gets you closer to the top. To take the next step, you must completely leave behind the step you are on. Do you stop and hang on to each step before you let go? You know where you are going and that knowledge will allow you to let go and continue forward.

Learn where you are going. Know that you are on the right step. Catch the vision of tomorrow, it may never be easy, but you will make it easier by learning to say "Good-bye."

When you say good-bye to the burdens of the past, you now can truly look forward.

NUGGETS FOR THE MIND...

> There comes a time for all of us
> When we must say good-bye,
> Can never, never die,
> Although the curtain falls at last
> Is that a cause to grieve?
> The future's fairer than the past
> If only we believe
> And trust in God's eternal care --
> So when the Master calls
> Let's say that life is still more fair
> Although the curtain falls.
> --Author Unknown

"One must never lose time in vainly regretting the past nor in complaining about the changes which cause us discomfort, for change is the very essence of life."
 --Anatole France

"In order to climb to a higher level, you must say good-bye to the level you are on."
 --Sam Spencer

"There are times when forgetting can be just as important as remembering -- and even more difficult."
 --Author Unknown

#82 INVOLVE OTHERS IN REACHING YOUR GOALS

Your world is full of people who have a great deal more experience than you in whatever you're doing. These are people you hope will be happy to help you along. Without involving others, your journey through life will be slow, arduous, and lonely. There are those who are willing to lend a hand. Seek them out! Allow others to help!

Involving others in reaching your goals helps maintain the motivation to keep you going. They can encourage and help you stay on the right track. They can also help with new and diverse ideas to solve your problems. Your burdens become lighter when others help you along the way.

The story is told of a man who had a dream where he visited both heaven and hell. He first went to hell where he saw a large banquet table full of delicious food. Each person had a four foot long knife and had a four foot long fork. However, he noticed the people were thin and wasting away. In heaven he saw the same sight, a beautiful banquet table full of delicious food. People had the same four foot long knives and forks. However, the people were all well fed, they were feeding each other, thereby feeding themselves.

When you involve others, they encourage you and make sure you reach your goals. Involve others, take the risk. You will find the risk ultimately worth it.

NUGGETS FOR THE MIND . . .

"Socrates said, 'Know thyself'. Cicero said, 'Control Thyself'. Jesus said 'Give of thyself'."
--Author Unknown

"What we seek we shall find; what we flee from flees from us;...and hence the high caution, that, since we are sure of having what we wish, we beware to ask only for high things."
--Ralph Waldo Emerson

Consult your friend on all things, especially on those which respect yourself. His counsel may then be useful when your own self-love might impair your judgment."
--Seneca

"Every man who is high up loves to think that he has done it all by himself; and the wife smiles and lets it go at that."
--James Matthew Barrimore

"If you really want to achieve your goals, let the world know where you are going, they will either push you along or you will drag them all the way."
--Sam Spencer

"You can't help someone get up a hill without getting closer to the top yourself."
--General H. Norman Schwarzkopf

#83   GIVE DAILY AFFIRMATIONS TO THOSE YOU LIVE WITH

Giving daily affirmations is using positive statements that build self-esteem. When you give affirmations to others they should be given in such a way that they build their self-esteem. Such expressions should be sincere and in a spirit which conveys that you believe in the other person and that you care about them.

Here are some examples of affirmations you might consider:

...You are a fun person to be around.
...Your smile warms the whole room.
...I'm glad you are my friend.
...You can do it.
...If anyone can, you can.
...You deserve a happy life.

You will find that when you get out of the habit of giving affirmations that friendships become strained, and potentially lost. A few words to express approval of their actions is all that is required. If you have trouble thinking of things you might say, ask a close friend for suggestions. Also remember what affirmations you have received from others that made you feel good and then give similar expressions of approval and confirmation to others.

I have given you a few ideas to help you get started. Create your own. Choose someone at home, in the office, or just anywhere and think of a few positive things you can say, then say them. Do this for a different person each day. You will make a difference.

NUGGETS FOR THE MIND . . .

"Parents can plant magic in a child's mind through certain words spoken with some thrilling quality of voice, some uplift of the heart."
 --Robert MacNeil

"Learn how to pay compliments. Start with the members of your family, and you will find it will become easier later in life to compliment others. It's a great asset."
 --Letitia Baldrige

"Don't tell a woman she's pretty; tell her there's no other woman like her, and all roads will open to you."
 --Jules Renard

"Keep away from people who try to belittle your ambitions. Small people always do that, but the really great make you feel that you, too, can become great."
 --Mark Twain

My Creed
I would be true, for there are those who trust me;
   I would be pure, for there are those who care;
I would be strong, for there is much to suffer;
   I would be brave, for there is much to dare.
I would be friend to all, the foe, the friendless;
   I would be giving and forget the gift;
I would be humble, for I know my weakness;
   I would look up, and laugh, and love, and lift.
 --Harold Arnold Walter

#84 VISUALIZE SUCCESS

Think of yourself as the creator of your destiny. Look into your future. Ask yourself, "What do I want to become?" "How do I visualize the successes I will have?" If you can't form a vivid picture, you will have a very difficult time recognizing the destination when you arrive there.

I have a friend who is a wood carver. He picks up a unique piece of wood and visualizes what he is going to carve from that piece of wood. He doesn't just start whittling away until he can see in his mind, the vision of what he is going to create.

Visualize yourself in the success corner of life. Visualize yourself on the gold medal platform. Before you start any task, visualize where you are and how you will get there. See yourself from start to finish. This does two things, first it gives your subconscious a clear picture so it can deal with past experiences and bring them to the forefront as you encounter problems and formulate a plan. Second, it helps intensify the desire to succeed because you have already vicariously experienced success.

If you want to know where you will be in the future, visualize that destination today and work toward the vision. Remember that the mind cannot achieve anything it does not understand. You must visualize your success until it becomes clear. Visualize daily what, where, and how you will succeed. Get the picture! Visualize success!

NUGGETS FOR THE MIND . . .

"In every block of marble I see a statue, see it as plainly as though it stood before me, shaped and perfect in attitude and action. I have only to hew away the rough walls to reveal it to other eyes as mine already see it."
 --Michelangelo

"Nothing can stop people with the right attitudes from achieving their goals."
 --Author Unknown

"The opportunities of man are limited by only his imagination. But so few have imagination that there are ten thousand fiddlers to one composer."
 --Charles F. Kettering

"It is not the mountain we conquer but ourselves."
 --Edmund Hillary

"In the long run men hit only what they aim at."
 --Henry David Thoreau

"Your image determines your success. Continually project the image you would like to become, and in time, you will become the image you project."
 --Sam Spencer

#85   LIVE WITH LESS THAN PERFECTION

I'm not against perfection, but I question perfectionism. Having things perfect may help you feel happy for the short term. When things have attained your supposed state of perfection, you will find yourself spending most of the balance of your time trying to maintain this perfection. Lighten up! Get a life! Learn to enjoy things that are less than perfect. This is the real world.

The person who always demands that everything be perfect is not fun to be with. Some things are okay if they're not quite perfect. At home for example. Maybe everything in your kitchen isn't in its perfect place. Maybe the pictures on the wall are a tad crooked. Maybe there is a wrinkle on the bedspread. Does it really matter that much?

Here is a perfection gauge to help you:

   ...Can I accept things as they are?
   ...What would happen If I accepted things as they are?
   ...Is it actually important or just trivial?
   ...Is there a way I can be happy and accept things?

When I began to accept living with less than perfection in my life, I found my relationships with others improved. Particularly with my family. They were more open with me and felt less challenged by lofty expectations and could be themselves.

If you're caught up in perfectionism, try letting a few things that really don't matter slide each day. You will become more relaxed. In time your blood pressure will drop, you will find more inner peace - a peaceful reward.

NUGGETS FOR THE MIND . . .

"Perfectionism is the enemy of creation, as extreme self-solitude is the enemy of well-being."
 --John Updike

"Be patient with everyone, but above all with yourself."
 --St. Francis de Sales

"There is one piece of advice, in a life of study, which I think no one will object to; and that is, every now and then to be completely idle--to do nothing at all."
 --Sydney Smith

"If you expect perfection from people, your whole life is a series of disappointments, grumblings and complaints. If, on the contrary, you pitch your expectations low, taking folks as the inefficient creatures which they are, you are frequently surprised by having them perform better than you had hoped."
 --Bruce Barton

"If you aspire to the highest place, there is no disgrace to stop at the second, or even the third place."
 --Cicero

"When you aim for perfection, you discover it's a moving target."
 --George Fisher

#86 RECOGNIZE YOU CAN'T SAVE THE WORLD

There are those who would like to make everything right everywhere - at work, at home, in the neighborhood or wherever there is a problem. It would be nice if someone could save the world and solve all of its problems. This is idealistic and not very realistic or even practical.

Recognize that you cannot save the world. Many people hurt others, and are a negative part of the environment. They will always be here. You probably cannot change them. But you should help those whom you can influence. Help the people you can help, then move on. Answer the questions you can answer, then move on. Solve the problems you can solve, then move on.

Don't worry about the things you could have done. You can't always help a person who has chosen to be a moral deviant, nor can you make every place a pleasant place to be. The most important thing you can do is to help yourself first. Once you have good control over yourself, then reach out to those who are closest to you. Continue this process making larger circles as you progress. You may only be a single individual, but you can make a difference when you stand out and do something. All your little something's add up in time. And in time you will become the sum total of all your little differences.

You *can* make a difference. Improve *your* small portion of the world. Embark on a journey to help wherever and however you can. You will discover numerous welcome ports and gain innumerable life-long friends along the way.

NUGGETS FOR THE MIND...

"Forming resentments with mankind may be called 'planting misery'; putting aside virtuous deeds; instead of practicing them; may be called 'robbing oneself.'"
 --Wisdom of the Chinese

"When chickens quit quarreling over their food they often find that there is enough for all of them. I wonder if it might not be the same with the human race."
 --Don Marquis

"Man is not the creature of circumstances; circumstances are the creatures of man."
 --Benjamin Disraeli

"You can listen to what everybody says, but the fact remains that you've got to get out there and do the thing yourself."
 --Joan Sutherland

"Everyone thinks of changing the world, but no one thinks of changing himself."
 --Leo Tolstoy

"Do not commit the error, common among the young, of assuming that if you cannot save the whole of mankind, that you have failed."
 --Author Unknown

#87   STAY AWAY FROM NEGATIVE PEOPLE

Do you know people who pick everything positive apart and destroy the good feeling when they walk into a room? Stay away from those people. They can destroy your joy in life. It is difficult to perform well when you are with negative people. Invest some time in people who are positive. Build friendships and relationships that are both positive and constructive.

You choose your friends. You choose how long you will be with them. You choose how you will let them influence you. Review the friends you have, then ask yourself, "Does this person generally uplift me or does he give me negative feelings?" If your associates bring out your negative self, you should consider getting new associates, especially if you are looking for a happier, more successful self.

I have a friend who was telling about his new place of employment. His employer allows no negative talk in staff meetings, in dealing with customers, or anywhere at work. All managers are trained in being positive with employees and customers alike. My friend went on to tell me what a pleasant, productive atmosphere this environment provides. What a great contrast to his many years of employment in offices where everyone was negative. He too has become a much more positive person, thanks to those around him.

Remember that your environment influences how you feel and what you become. You can't afford negative influence. Eliminate as much of the negative as possible! This will certainly increase your effectiveness through positive power in thought and in action.

NUGGETS FOR THE MIND . . .

"Don't make friends who are comfortable to be with. Make friends who will force you to lever yourself up."
 --Thomas J. Watson Sr.

"Above all do not talk yourself out of good ideas by trying to expound then at haphazard gatherings."
 --Jacques Barzum

"Dwell not upon thy weariness, thy strength shall be according to the measure of thy desire."
 --Arab Proverb

"Esteem has more engaging charms than friendship and even love. It captivates hearts better, and never makes ingrates."
 --Francois de La Rochefoucauld

"The super-salesman neither permits his subconscious mind to "broadcast" negative thoughts nor give expression to them through words, for the reason that he understands that "like attracts like" and negative suggestions attract negative action and negative decisions from prospective buyers."
 --Napoleon Hill

#88   USE SELF TALK - GIVE YOURSELF DAILY AFFIRMATIONS

Give yourself daily affirmations. If no one else will do it for you, do it for yourself. There are those who will say that this is arrogant, egotistical, or self-centered. This may be so, but I tell you this, you need to hear these kinds of affirmations!

Say to yourself, "I can do it!" "I will make it work!" "I like who I am!" "I am a great employee, father, husband, mother, wife!" "I have great value!" "There is nobody like me!" "I'm Good!" "What a good job I did!" Keep talking to yourself, no one knows better than you what positive affirmations you need to hear.

When suddenly being faced with an incurable illness, I had to form a foundation that would be uplifting and positive. I began to talk to myself. In the mornings I said to myself, "You will do better today than yesterday." Then I began to say, "You can handle this." Then after several months of self talk, adjusting attitude and lifestyle, one morning it all came together, I felt that I had conquered my situation. I looked into the mirror and said, "Watch out world, Sam Spencer is back!"

How important it is to give yourself the encouragement and strength you need by simple, sincere self-talk. Learn how to make self-talk a positive part of your life. Think of yourself as "your best friend from within," then listen to what you have to say.

At times you may find this step slow going, some situations cannot change. However, do it anyway, to do nothing is going nowhere at all!

NUGGETS FOR THE MIND . . .

"Your ability to use the principle of autosuggestion will depend, very largely, upon your capacity to concentrate upon a given desire until that desire becomes a burning obsession."
 --Napoleon Hill

"The key to every man is his thought. . . . He can only be reformed by showing him a new idea which commands his own."
 --Ralph Waldo Emerson

"A desire can overcome all objections and obstacles."
 --Gunderson

"Let each day be your masterpiece."
 --Author Unknown

"Tell yourself what you need to hear and before long you will be living it."
 --Sam Spencer

"When you cannot get a compliment any other way pay yourself one."
 --Mark Twain

#89 HELP OTHERS SAVE FACE

Everyone can be a little thoughtless or reckless from time to time. You may find yourself in an awkward situation and not quite know how to get out. You can become more successful in your relationships with others if you will help others save face when you see they are in a tight spot or predicament. Put yourself in their particular situation and ask yourself, "What would I like others to say, or how might I appreciate a helping hand?" Then go ahead and do it!

I have been in the position where I forgot someone's name and was embarrassed that I had forgotten it. As we met again later, begging their pardon, I was greatly relieved when he would say something like, "I know how you feel, I forget names too." This kindness helped me to save face and my respect for that person increased.

Here are some ideas and phrases you may find helpful:

...Instead of "You broke that," try, "It looks like it's broken"
...Put yourself in the category with the other person -- "I often do the very same thing."
...Help others feel it will be OK -- "This sort of thing happens all the time."
...Find a way to refer to the event without personally including the individual.

There are many ways to help someone save face. Now that you have learned this concept, find other ways of helping other save face. Be observant and thoughtful then practice your new skill. You will develop deeper friendships as you extend your hand of kindness.

NUGGETS FOR THE MIND...

"Nothing is there more friendly to a man than a friend in need."
  --Plautus

"He that does good for good's sake seeks neither praise nor reward, but he is sure of both in the end."
  --William Penn

"In the long run, if it isn't a win for both of us, we both lose."
  --Steven R. Covey

"You can make more friends in a month by being interested in them than in ten years by trying to get them interested in you."
  --Charles Allen

"When guests stay too long, try treating them like members of the family. If they don't leave then, they never will."
  --Martin Ragaway

"He that does good for good's sake seeks neither praise nor reward, but he is sure of both in the end."
  --William Penn

#90   DON'T LOSE SIGHT OF YOUR OBJECTIVE

Your objective is the most important part of success. It is your destination. If you don't know where you are going, you will never know when you get there. You will be running around in circles. When you lose sight of your objective you begin to spend time in other areas or on projects that take you away from your objective. And if you do get where you wanted to go, it will be by chance. Don't leave life to chance!

To illustrate this, cover your eyes with a blind fold. Now try to walk a straight line. You may walk fairly straight, but you will do much better if you can keep your eyes on the goal. Stay focused on your objective.

On several occasions a friend of mine gave me a ride in his airplane. When we were in the sky, he would allow me to take the controls. I would fly with no direction at all, like a child aimlessly wandering in a field. The only time I had any direction was when I went back to the airport to land. When I would head back to the airport I flew toward landmarks that eventually guided me to the airstrip. When I took my eyes off the landmarks, I drifted off course. Then, when focusing once again on my objective, invariably I corrected the direction of the plane until I was back on course. I learned that the longer I looked away the more correction was needed and that some correction was always necessary.

Don't go in circles, keep your eyes on your objective. In your journey through life, you will continually need to make minor adjustments. Make them, keep focused and you will stay on course.

NUGGETS FOR THE MIND . . .

"There are admirable potentialities in every human being. Believe in your strength and your youth. Learn to repeat endlessly to yourself 'It all depends on me.''
 --Andre Gide

"Keep your eyes pointed straight ahead, neither to the right nor to the left. That's the shortest way to get where you are going."
 --Sam Spencer

"If your determination is fixed, do not counsel you to despair. Few things are im to diligence and skill. Great works are performed not by strength, but by perseverance."
 --Samuel Johnson

If you built castles in the air, your work need not be lost; that is where they should be. Now put the foundation under them."
 --David Henry Thoreau

"When I look back I remember how hard it has been, but when I look forward, I remember where I want to go."
 --Sam Spencer

#91 LEARN SOMETHING NEW EACH DAY

Never stop learning. One would like to think this is simple that you always are learning. But take a minute and ask yourself, "What did I learn yesterday?" Most people have a hard time thinking of something specific that they learned yesterday unless they are a student (Some of them have a hard time too).

This will take a conscious effort. Before you go to bed try asking yourself, "What did I learn today?" Each morning ask yourself, "What do I want to learn today?" Notice I said, "want." You can decide what you learn. What a novel idea! Set a plan each morning to learn something new that day and make it something you need or want to learn.

Here are some ways to be sure you are learning something new daily:

   ...Keep reading this book and practice the principles.
   ...Browse through the dictionary, encyclopedia or some reference material.
   ...Watch educational shows on TV or listen to them on the radio.
   ...Ask others what they have learned, then listen to the answer.
   ...Attend seminars and classes.
   ...Read books that will teach you new skills.

Teach your family and others to recognize the value of learning by sharing with them things you have learned. Make a conscious effort to expand your knowledge. Make this a daily ritual. Set a daily goal not to retire until you have reasonably fed your mind.

NUGGETS FOR THE MIND . . .

"Where there is much desire to learn, there, of necessity, will be much arguing, much writing, many opinions; for opinion in good men is but knowledge in the making."
--John Milton

"Hungering and striving after knowledge, is what makes a scholar; hungering and striving after virtue is what makes a Saint; hungering and striving after noble action is what makes a hero and a man."
--Orison Swett Marden

"Education, then, beyond all other devices of human origin, is the great equalizer of the conditions of men, -- the balance-wheel of the social machinery."
--Horace Mann

"Since we cannot know all that is to be known of everything, we ought to know a little about everything."
--Blaise

"Anyone can make a mistake. A fool insists on repeating it."
--Robertine Maynard

#92 START EARLY IN THE MORNING

I have heard it said, "If you want to find out who is going places, get up early in the morning." Join the early morning club of movers and shakers; shake off the covers early in the morning and get moving!

I will get more done by noon when I start working at six or seven in the morning than when I start at nine and work to six or seven in the evening. You will find fewer interruptions and distractions. Because it is quiet and peaceful in the morning, your concentration is better. Your efficiency and creativity will increase because you are more alert. And best of all, you will have your work done early enough to have some time left for yourself. Use this extra time to do things for yourself, for your family, or maybe even towards making yourself more productive in your career.

If you have a job that will not allow you to start early, still get up early and do the things you would have done after getting home. You will come home without the burden of many undone tasks hanging over your head. Your time will be freed up to do other things. You will have more time for your family and for yourself. If you work at home, still get started early. You will find more energy, you too will gain more time for yourself, and develop positive attitude changes that will slowly work into your life as you enjoy this success.

This is one way to work both harder and smarter!

NUGGETS FOR THE MIND . . .

"The largest barrier to success is removing the mattress from one's back in the morning."
--Author Unknown

"Sloth makes all things difficult; but Industry, all easy; and he that rises late must trot all day and scarce overtake his business at night; while Laziness travels so slowly that Poverty soon overtakes him."
--Benjamin Franklin

"The bed is a bundle of paradoxes: we go to it with reluctance, yet we quit it with regret; we make up our minds every night to leave it early, but we make up our bodies every morning to keep it late."
--Colton

"Early to bed and early to rise, Makes a man healthy, wealthy, and wise."
--Benjamin Franklin

"To keep up with the movers and shakers, you must shake off the covers and get moving early!"
--Sam Spencer

"Believe me, you have to get up early if you want to get out of bed."
--Groucho Marx

#93   LIVE YOUR DREAMS TODAY

Everyone has dreams. Dreams make life fun and interesting. Anyone who does or becomes anything, first had a dream. Once a dream is acted upon, things begin to happen. Keep it up and you will get where you want to go.

You have heard it said, "There's no time like the present." "Do it now." And I say this, "If you wait until all the ducks are in line before you go hunting, you'll never go hunting." If you've always wanted to do something, what's stopping you? Get in gear! Just do it!

Remember the story of Walt Disney? Mr. Disney had a dream. He acted on his dream and anyone can tell you the rest of the story. Your expectations may not be as grand. Even though your dreams may be small, they are all yours. So begin to work on them. Think of how you can initiate implementation today. Plan, then act!

Do something about your dreams today. You will find more joy and satisfaction in your life because you are doing what *you* want to do. If you wait, things will change and you might never get started. You will need to organize and plan to incorporate new ideas into your life. When you work on *your* dreams, you will have greater enthusiasm and this will transfer to all other areas of your life.

Remember: Every great success story first started as a dream!

Everyday *do* something about *your* dreams!

NUGGETS FOR THE MIND . . .

"Coach to Jesse Owens who wanted to be 'The fastest man in the world, the greatest runner.' -- You must have a dream and a ladder to that dream.
        1st rung is DETERMINATION
        2nd rung is DEDICATION
        3rd rung is DISCIPLINE
        4th rung is ATTITUDE
The first three rungs are important, but the fourth rung is vital."
  --Jesse Owens' Coach

     If you can imagine it,
       You can achieve it,
     If you can dream it,
       You can become it.
          -- Author Unknown

"Like dreams, small creeks grow into mighty rivers."
  --Author Unknown

"It's not the dream that makes the man, it's the man that makes the dream."
  --Sam Spencer

#94 WORK HARDER AND SMARTER

You have heard it said many times, " work smarter." This is good advice. I have also heard it said, "work harder." That too is wise advice. I suggest you take it another step; do both at the same time. Work harder and smarter. Why stop half way? It's true that as you grow older, you may slow down in some areas. But you also become more efficient. Recognize your strengths and capitalize on them. Why give less than your best?

Be creative in finding more efficient ways to do things. For some reason, as people grow older they sometimes allow their creative abilities to lay dormant. Why? Who made these people feel less creative? Why did they even believe the intimidator? Creativity is a skill and you need to keep practiced to stay sharp.

In my manufacturing business, I designed several production systems that allowed me to manufacture my products faster and with a higher quality than my competitors. Often they would comment that they couldn't believe I was able to manufacture product at such a low cost. I was constantly thinking of ways to become more efficient. By designing more efficient production systems, I could produce more product in less time. Just because you may become more efficient is no reason to not work as hard. In fact, just the opposite is true.

Anyone can work harder. Creative people work smarter. To be a highly successful person you must work both harder and smarter.

NUGGETS FOR THE MIND . . .

"The tallest trees are most in the power of the winds, and ambitious men of the blasts of fortune."
 --Penn

"Ambition is so powerful a passion in the human breast, that however high we reach we are never satisfied."
 --Machiavelli

"You may be disappointed if you fail, but you are doomed if you don't try."
 --Beverly Sills

"We must not promise what we ought not, lest we be called on to perform what we cannot."
 --Abraham Lincoln

"You cannot dream yourself into a character; you must hammer and forge one for yourself."
 --Froude

"When you play, play hard; when you work don't play at all."
 --Theodore Roosevelt

#95   HELP MAKE OTHERS COMFORTABLE

Have you ever been in a situation where you felt awkward, or out of place? Maybe you wanted to get out of the situation and couldn't. How would you have felt if someone had come to you and made you feel more comfortable? Why don't you do this for others?

Here are some situations and ways you can help make someone feel more comfortable:

- ...A new employee at work -- Have a conversation with her and ask her about herself. Show her around or even eat lunch with her.
- ...At a social gathering -- Introduce that particular person to the most influential person you are acquainted with at the gathering.
- ...An embarrassing situation -- Find a way to help her become more comfortable, ask yourself two things:
  ..What would I like to have done for me?
  ..How can I help her save face?

This is a trait that requires you to develop compassion and a caring for others. You will need to be more observant of those around you. You will have to take some risk in reaching out. As you stretch you will grow.

When you make this a habit, your life will become happier. You cannot show kindness and compassion to others without increased personal fulfillment. The next time you see someone standing alone, go stand beside them, have a sincere conversation, and to make them feel especially good talk about them!

NUGGETS FOR THE MIND . . .

"A good deed is never lost. He who sows courtesy, reaps friendship; he who plants kindness, gathers love; pleasure bestowed upon a grateful mind was never sterile, but generally gratitude begets reward."
 --Basil

>Somebody did a golden deed;
>Somebody proved a friend in need;
>Somebody sang a beautiful song;
>Somebody smiled the whole day long;
>Somebody thought, 'Tis sweet to live;'
>Somebody said, 'I'm glad to give;'
>Somebody fought a valiant fight;
>Somebody lived to shield the right;
>   Was that 'somebody' you?
>   --Author Unknown

"Kindness is a language which the deaf can hear and blind can read. "
 --Mark Twain

"You may be sorry that you spoke, sorry you stayed or went, sorry you won or lost, sorry so much was spent. But as you go through life, you'll find — you're never sorry you were kind."
 --Herbert V. Prochnow

#96   RECOGNIZE THERE ARE SEVERAL WAYS TO ACHIEVE THE SAME RESULTS

There are many avenues to achieve the goal. Some may choose paths different from you. That is okay! When I finally grasped this concept, my life and relationships really became simpler. In a problem solving workshop to illustrate this point, I had everyone form into small groups of 4 or 5. Each group was given a United States Map. They were told they were to leave Salt Lake City and travel to Washington DC. They had 3 weeks to get there, and had to travel at least 50 miles each day. The task was to come to a consensus on the route and the places to see along the way. 20 minutes was allotted to do this.

Each group took different routes, visited different sights, but they all arrived at Washington DC on time. Could this example apply to your life? How many ways are there to do the right thing? How many roads "lead to Rome?"

One day I needed a prototype built of a new product I had designed. With no time to build it myself, I asked my top employee to accept the challenge. After a complete explanation he took my drawings and went to work. In time he returned, prototype in hand, exactly as I had envisioned the product. He reviewed his production procedure with me -- not exactly the way I would have done it, but had achieved the desired results. That's OK!

I learned that when you let others follow the path they are most comfortable with, you both win. The more you can accept the path others have chosen to achieve success, the more success you both will enjoy.

NUGGETS FOR THE MIND . . .

"It were not best that we should all think alike; it is difference of opinion that makes horse-races."
 --Mark Twain

"The difference between a neurotic, a psychotic, and a psychiatrist. The neurotic builds castles in the sky, the psychotic lives in them and the psychiatrist collects the rent."
 --Author Unknown

"In proportion as our own mind is enlarged we discover a greater number of men of originality. Commonplace people see no difference between one man and another."
 --Pascal

"There are many truths of which the full meaning cannot be realized until personal experience has brought it home."
 --John Stuart Mill

"Never tell people how to do things. Tell them what to do and they will surprise you with their ingenuity"
 --Author Unknown

#97   DON'T DWELL ON WHAT DIDN'T WORK

When something absolutely doesn't work, it doesn't work! This is just like kicking the proverbial dead horse. Just bury it!

Here is the problem with dwelling on what doesn't work; *it's negative!* To have increased success, you have to eliminate the negative from your life. Whenever you expend negative energy, you are going in reverse. Spend too much time with negative thoughts and you will have a long way to go to get back where you ought to be. Change gears to positive and get going forward. Get on to the next task. Quit discussing what didn't work.

Thomas Edison held 1,093 patents. You have him to thank for the light bulb that allows you to read this book. One day he was asked about the 25,000 experiments that he attempted while he was working on the storage battery. Mr. Edison insisted that he had not failed, he had succeeded in finding 24,999 ways a storage battery would not work.

So if it doesn't work, learn quickly, don't dwell on it. Just move on to what works!

NUGGETS FOR THE MIND . . .

"I never think about the past, only about the present and the future, and I always conceive of myself as growing. I have never had one second of boredom since I was born."
 --Mary Martin

"The past has its place and is valuable for lessons learned. The present also has its place, and what we cannot change should not needlessly keep us from looking and moving forward. Nothing lost or left behind should keep us from now becoming what we can become, from learning what we now can learn."
 --Richard L. Evans

"The most valuable thing I have learned from life is to regret nothing."
 --Somerset Maugham

"Don't be afraid of growing slowly, be afraid of standing still."
 --Chinese Proverb

"Once you've failed, analyze the problem and find out why, because each failure is one more step leading up to the cathedral of success. The only time you don't want to fail is the last time you try."
 --Charles F. Kettering

#98   LOOK IN THE MIRROR EACH DAY AND PRACTICE BEING NICE

If you want to know how you appear to others, take time to look in the mirror. Greet yourself, observe how you do it, practice your technique. Examine your smile and polish it. Is it pleasant? Pick other mannerisms that you can improve and practice them in the mirror each day.

Each morning as you finish preparing to leave for work, look in the mirror and smile. Reach out as if to shake your hand and begin to rehearse the events you have planned for that day. Talk to the person in the mirror in a pleasant way. Smile at him. Practice asking questions you might ask to someone that day. This practice will do two things for you. First, you will feel better about yourself and self-confidence will increase because of the positive minutes you are spending. Second, when you meet others you will have practiced being nice and automatically you will become what you have practiced.

This idea is very simple, and I can promise you that it will bring you greater success in your dealings with other people. Greater success with others can't help but make your life a little happier.

Try this: The next time you are going to a business appointment, arrive early, run into the rest room, look in the mirror and practice your greeting and your smile. You could even use the mirror in your car! This little routine will make a difference. Just try it, you will find that it actually works!

NUGGETS FOR THE MIND . . .

"Confidence and courage come through preparation and practice."
 --Author Unknown

"If you want a trait, act as if you already have the trait."
 --William James

"For as he thinketh in his heart, so is he..."
 --Proverbs 23:7

"Look well to thyself; there is a source of strength which will always spring up if thou wilt always look there."
 --Marcus Aurelius

"Know thyself' means this, that you get acquainted with what you know, and what you do."
 --Menender of Athens

"What you want to be eventually, that you must be every day; and by and by the quality of your deeds will get down into your soul."
 --Frank Crane

#99   BE A PROBLEM SOLVER

If you see a problem and you can solve it, *solve it!* If you can improve the path for another, *improve it!* If you can make life easier for another, *make it easier!* When you solve problems for yourself and for others, you will find an inner peace and satisfaction that cannot be equaled.

The story is told of a king who ordered all his subjects to build a great highway across his kingdom. Upon completion, the king declared a special holiday in the kingdom. All his subjects were to participate in a race to the end of the highway and back to the castle. A great prize would be given to him who traveled the highway best. The morning of the race arrived. Everyone lined up to start the race, young and old, fast and slow. At mid day the faster runners began to cross the finish line. Late into the afternoon people were still finishing the great race. Long after the sun had gone down the final runner crossed the finish line. He went to the king with a large bag of gold. The elderly gentleman apologized to the king for his delay. He stated that when he got to the end of the highway there was a pile of debris the workers had left behind. He had stopped to clean it up and found the bag of gold at the bottom and could the king return it to the rightful owner. The king said, "You are the rightful owner, he who makes a traveled road better for the next is he who travels the road best."

Learn from this story that the greatest rewards come to those who solve problems. To withhold your knowledge when it will make someone else's life better or neglect to assist one in need, is purely selfish. Freely give and you receive so much more in return!

NUGGETS FOR THE MIND . . .

"We grow by being able to tackle the process rather than resist it"
 --Steven R. Covey

"Try to put into practice what you already know, and in so doing you will in good time discover the hidden things which you now inquire about."
 --Henry Van Dyke

"When a person is down in the world, an ounce of help is better than a pound of preaching."
 --Edward Bulwer-Lytton

"There is a vast difference between putting your nose into other people's business and putting your heart into people's problems."
 --Author Unknown

"If you cannot lift the load of another's back, do not walk away. Try to lighten it."
 --Frank Tyger

"Have you got a problem? Do what you can where you are with what you've got."
 --Theodore Roosevelt

#100 STOP SAYING "POOR ME" AND SAY "RICH ME"

Many people look at what they don't have and never really look at what they actually do have. Every day take some time to look at what you DO have and appreciate where you are and what you have.

If you have a problem being thankful for what you have, no matter if you have much or if you have little, try doing the following exercise:

Get a pencil and a piece of paper then walk around your house and make a list of the things that make your life easier or more comfortable. Include those things that make you happy or help you relax. This list could include items such as your house, your sofa, your bed, your refrigerator, or even your beat up old car. Now get even deeper into this project and include things such as your friends(by name), your family, education, job, and other intimate elements of your life.

Once you have completed a lengthy list, take time to review it and answer this question for each item, "What would I do without this item or person?" "What would my family life be like?" "Where would I be?" This is not a question of could you survive without such with less, it is an exercise to develop recognition and awareness.

As your attitude and perspective changes, you will soon see that you really are a rich person after all. There may be some things you would like to change, this is always the case. However, your gratitude for what you *do* have will multiply and you will begin to feel very fortunate. Your heart will become open and soften – and more is always given to the person with a soft, open heart.

NUGGETS FOR THE MIND . . .

"Govern thyself then you will be able to govern the world."
--Author Unknown

"Know yourself, master yourself, conquest of self is most gratifying."
--Author Unknown

"Self mastery comes through denial of the little things."
--Author Unknown

"You've first got to have faith in yourself before you can do anything."
--Sterling W. Sill

"Self Resolve to know thyself and know he that finds himself loses his misery."
--Author Unknown

"Good thoughts bear good fruit, bad thoughts bear bad fruits and man is his own gardener."
--James Allen

#101 GIVE YOURSELF THE RESPECT YOU DESERVE

What is respect? Respect is reverence or esteem for something or someone great; to hold in high or special regard. If you have respect for someone you honor them, you praise them, you stand-up for them and you don't allow others to abuse them or injure them. You, indeed, are someone great! You are special and unique! Within you are the abilities to become even greater!

Self-respect is nothing more than standing up for yourself and requiring the reverence you deserve. Don't let people take advantage of you or abuse you because you may be weaker in some way. Be faithful to yourself, don't accept degrading or improper treatment of yourself from others.

One day I was in a sales situation where the prospect became abusive and began to challenge, unreasonably, my company, myself and my product. It was obvious that he was not just trying to gain a better understanding of the services I offered. Realizing that I, too, had a choice; closing my briefcase, I politely stated, "I don't think we can do business," and then walked out.
Don't let anyone, no matter who they are, require you to go against your personal values. No other person, no job or position is worth the loss of your self-respect. It is difficult to do and be your best when you allow others to diminish your self-worth.

If you have done a good job, recognize it. If some one disputes you, stand up for yourself. Recognize what and who you are. Expect, and require from others, and especially from yourself, the respect you deserve!

NUGGETS FOR THE MIND . . .

"Never violate the sacredness of your individual self-respect"
 --Theodore Parker

"Human rights rest on human dignity. The dignity of man is an ideal worth fighting for and worth dying for."
 --Robert Maynard

"It is necessary to the happiness of man that he be mentally faithful to himself."
 --Thomas Paine

"The best thing to give to your enemy is forgiveness; to an opponent, tolerance; to a friend, your heart; to your child, a good example; to a father, deference; to your mother, conduct that will make her proud of you; to yourself, respect; to all men, charity."
 --Mrs. Balfour

"It is difficult to make a man miserable while he feels he is worthy of himself and claims kindred to the great God who made him."
 --Abraham Lincoln

"A human being's first responsibility is to shake hands with himself."
 --Author Unknown

"Probably the most neglected friend you have is you."
 --Author Unknown